CERAMIC
FORM

PETER LANE

CERAMIC
FORM

Design and Decoration

PETER LANE

COLLINS

To Freda Margaret Lane

First published in 1988 by
William Collins Sons & Co., Ltd
London · Glasgow · Sydney
Auckland · Toronto · Johannesburg

© Peter Lane 1988

Designer: Caroline Hill
Art Director: Janet James
Illustrator: Tig Sutton

**British Library Cataloguing in
Publication Data**

Lane, Peter, *1932–*
Ceramic form
1. Pottery 2. Porcelain
I. Title
738.2   NK4225

ISBN 0 00 412102 3

Set in Linotron Sabon
by Ace Filmsetting Ltd,
Frome, Somerset
Originated, printed and bound in
Hong Kong
by South China Printing Co.

Title page: Three porcelain bowls,
incised and inlaid with coloured
porcelains, unglazed, and polished with
silicon carbide paper. Fired to 1260°C.
By PETER LANE (UK), 1985.

CONTENTS

Acknowledgements

I am especially grateful to all the potters in the book who have so generously contributed photographs with details of their working methods and sources of inspiration. I am also indebted to my editor, Caroline Churton and the designer, Caroline Hill for their thoroughness and patience throughout the production of this book.

In addition, I would like to thank the following photographers, organizations and museums who have kindly granted permission for their photographs to be reproduced in this book:

J. M. Anderson, p. 72; David Annandale, p. 55; Robert Aude, pp. 34, 105, 122; R. Aulsebrook, pp. 76, 198; John Austin, pp. 12, 49, 136; Bill Backuber, p. 29; Richard Ball, pp. 150, 157; Hugo Barclay, p. 186; J. P. Beaudin, p. 68; Curtis Benzle, pp. 155, 156; Kjartan Bjelland, pp. 67, 141; E. Böhm, pp. 109, 115; Wolf Böwig, pp. 25, 152; Richard Burkett, p. 61; Castle Museum, Norwich, p. 57; City Museum, Stoke-on-Trent, pp. 8, 15, 21, 33, 45, 53, 92, 109, 181; John Coles, pp. 137, 181; Peter Colville, p. 79; Jane Coper, p. 58; Crafts Council, pp. 30, 81, 118, 162, 168, 176; David Cripps, p. 156; Pat Cumming, p. 65; B. Deller-Leppert, p. 80; Sharon Devaux, p. 28; C. M. Dixon, p. 158; Matthew Donaldson, pp. 127, 183; Antje Doss, p. 42; Andrew Dowsett, p. 179; Willi Faahsen, p. 33; Edith Farri, p. 177; Richard Faughn, p. 51; Paul Finlay, p. 34; Ron Forth, p. 65; Foto Strenger, pp. 20, 39; Foto-studio Baumann, pp. 56, 114, 123; Dan Gabriel, p. 62; Mogens Gad, p. 152; D. Gibson, p. 77; Jöunous Gilder, p. 96; Gertrud Glasgow, pp. 120, 170; Bernd P. Göbbels, pp. 47, 131, 144, 148; Chris Goddard, p. 98; Brian Goodman, pp. 24, 46; Dagmar Grauel, pp. 86, 113; Lawrence Gresswell, pp. 89, 199; Kenneth Grundy, p. 160; *The Guardian*, p. 98; Grant Hancock, pp. 44, 117, 163; Claire Henze, pp. 91, 153; Udo Hesse, pp. 51, 101; Leonard Hessing, pp. 104, 127; Tim Hill, pp. 16, 118; William Hunt, p. 96; Henry Jolles, p. 194; Paco Junquera, p. 87; Ray Kinnane, pp. 56, 128; Bernd Kirtz, pp. 86, 123, 147; Michael Kluvanek, pp. 41, 44, 94, 134, 167; Dr Paul Köster, p. 159; Landesgewerbeamt, p. 43; Anthony Lauro, p. 159; Jorge Mauricio, p. 23; Richard Muggleton, p. 56; Gail Reynolds Natzler, pp. 35, 118; Karen Norquay, pp. 103, 129, 151, 157; Dennis O'Hoy, p. 76; Dean Oshiro, pp. 79, 193; Paul Palau, pp. 23, 68, 69, 196; Rick Paulson, pp. 21, 60, 108, 131, 133, 147, 195; John Peacock, pp. 31, 118; Berry Perlus, p. 61; Anthony Phillips, p. 160; Jim Piper, pp. 9, 111, 146; Denis Rigault, p. 107; Röölesska Museum, Gothenburg, p. 96; Steve Rumsey, p. 149; Brian E. Rybolt, pp. 13, 67; Richard Sargent, p. 74; Jochen Schade, pp. 24, 27, 59, 67, 106, 115, 148, 158, 198; David Seed, p. 47; Seyok, pp. 50, 142; Pierre Soissons, pp. 39, 195; Hans-Joerg Soldan, p. 70; Warwick Sweeney, p. 102; Cornel Swen, p. 121; Teigens Fotoatelier, pp. 81, 104, 118, 119, 132, 135; Bill Thomas, p. 114; Ces Thomas, p. 86; Uellendahl, p. 138; S. Baker Vail, pp. 14, 172, 173; Wolfgang Waldow, p. 69; David Ward, pp. 85, 162; Cor Van Weele, pp. 116, 130; R. Wiech-Altdorf, pp. 19, 66, 100; Westminster Gallery, Boston, USA, p. 107; Andrew M. Whitlock, pp. 88, 116, 165; Howard Williams, pp. 69, 71, 128, 190, 192; John Wylie, pp. 45, 72, 101; Rolf Zwillsperger, pp. 77, 106, 191.

Pottery is at once the simplest and the most difficult of all the arts. It is the simplest because it is the most elemental; it is the most difficult because it is the most abstract. Historically it is among the first of the arts. The earliest vessels were shaped by hand from crude clay dug out of the earth, and such vessels were dried in the sun and wind. Even at that stage, before man could write, before he had a literature or even a religion, he had this art, and the vessels then made can still move us by their expressive form ... Judge the art of a country, judge the fineness of its sensibility, by its pottery; it is a sure touchstone. Pottery is pure art; it is art freed from any imitative intention.

Herbert Read, *The Meaning of Art*

1. INTRODUCTION

Originally, function alone dictated the form of pots. The most suitable shapes for particular applications evolved initially as simple, practical vessels intended for daily use. As skills and awareness developed, the natural human desire for ornamentation led not only to the refinement of pots regularly in use but also to increasingly elaborate forms and surface decoration. Sometimes, determined attempts were even made to disguise the mundane function of a vessel by imitating the form of an animal or plant, for example. But some of the finest shapes ever made are those which, with subtle variations, became common to many different cultures throughout the history of ceramics. Such pieces are timeless and their appeal seems likely to remain universal no matter what ingenuity potters of the future may summon up in aid of their work.

Clay has no form of its own, but its polymorphous nature presents the potter with a very wide choice of working methods by which to create forms of enormous variety. Yet despite this, a good number of those classical vessel shapes that evolved thousands of years ago are still being made, because they remain aesthetically satisfying. Many of these superb pots from ancient civilizations stand comparison favourably with good contemporary ceramics and would not seem out of place alongside the best of that which is exhibited in craft galleries today. Indeed, it is now virtually impossible to be totally original in making pottery vessels. Nuances of shape, combinations of colour, styles of decoration, and the relationship between these elements are the principal areas that offer the greatest scope for innovation.

It is hardly surprising, therefore, that certain familiar shapes continue to be explored by modern studio potters around the world, even though they find themselves surrounded by fresh, stimulating images from many quarters. In addition, they often face intense competition which brings further pressures to bear, so that some potters may be forced to make pieces of increasingly extravagant form and/or decoration in an attempt to be noticed. But it is the basically simple form which is most capable of infinitely subtle variation and expressive refinement. Hopefully, these unpretentious forms will continue to be admired and be received appreciatively by people everywhere, for it is generally acknowledged that even the most humble pots may possess qualities that can be recognized universally, thus transcending barriers of time, culture and language.

Some of those basic forms also survive in current industrial production with apparently little change in profile, rather like fine pieces of musical composition often heard but, perhaps, differing in style and performance. Nevertheless, with increased access to excellent technology and no role restrictions, potters are freer now than ever before to interpret their individual concept of the relationship between form and function or to reject

Bottle, bone china, possibly made by Minton, Stoke-on-Trent. Lustre decoration by Bernard Moore, Stoke-on-Trent, early 20th century.
(Photo: City Museum, Stoke-on-Trent)

Opposite: 'Catching the Dead'.
Wheel-thrown stoneware vase incised and decorated with iron, manganese and porcelain slips and glaze stains, fired to cone 5. The life cycle of the salmon which spawn in the Salmon River close to the potter's home in Oregon, USA, provides a constant source of stimulus for the drawing and decorative treatment of his work. Height 61 cm (24 in). By FRANK BOYDEN (USA), 1985. (Photo: Jim Piper)

Nerikomi bowl, hand-built with soft slices of multi-coloured porcelain joined together, stretched and shaped freehand, without the use of plaster moulds. 13×13 cm (5×5 in). By THOMAS HOADLEY (USA), 1984.

any such notion. This has fostered many exciting variations on familiar themes, but an overwhelming desire in modern society for visually striking or unusual objects often overlooks those more subtle qualities that do not depend on novelty for their existence. New or unfamiliar images affect our consciousness and may stimulate our thinking, but, if lacking in real substance, their impact is usually short-lived. Where originality (for its own sake) is allowed to become the sole aim of the potter, almost certainly the work will prove to be of no more than transitory value.

Why then do some pieces of pottery possess immortality while others do not? It is an unfortunate fact that a large proportion of the ceramics now produced suffers from a degree of shallowness and superficiality that contributes nothing to the continuing development of our ceramic heritage. To what extent could it be claimed that ideals of form and function were resolved so long ago and that all we can do today is make but minor modifications to profiles or decorative emphasis? Are there any truly revolutionary pottery forms being created by studio potters working today? What are the chances that our contemporary expressions will continue to satisfy human sensibilities and needs hundreds of years hence? I hope that some justifiable answers to such questions will be found in the pages of this book, not as printed statements, but through the reader's open-minded approach to both text and illustrations.

It is my intention in this book to explore a range of vessel forms, while keeping to a loosely defined theme of 'bottles' and 'bowls', in an attempt to identify some of those design elements which have made pottery an international language for the expression of feeling. I have chosen to restrict my subject matter to the two fundamental pottery forms of bowls and bottles because they provide the basis for an extremely large and varied body of

Stemmed porcelain bowl with a zinc barium glaze and copper oxide over. Fired in oxidation to cone 9 (1280°C). Height 13 cm (5 in). By RAY SILVERMAN (UK), 1985.

Opposite: 'Space Vessel' (cone series). With blue-green, sand-blasted glazes. Height 66 cm (26 in). By RICHARD HIRSCH (USA), 1985.

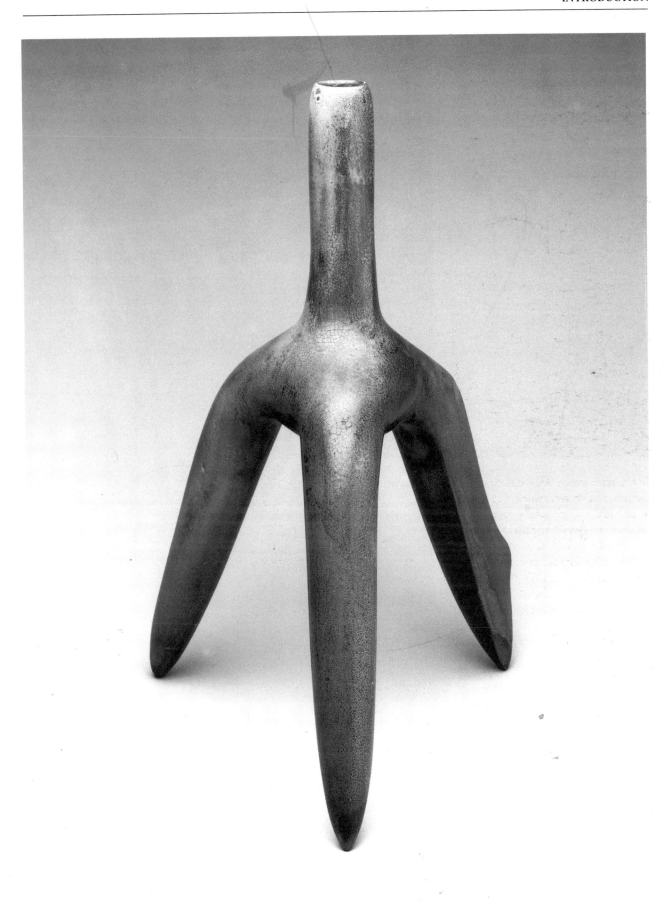

'Willow Weep 2'. Hand-built porcelain bowl constructed from coloured, inlaid sheets. Height 18 cm (7 in). By CURTIS AND SUZAN BENZLE (USA), 1985.

Porcelain bowl, wheel-thrown, turned, carved and fired unglazed to cone 9. Diameter 10 cm (4 in). By SANDRA BLACK (Australia), 1985. (Photo: John Austin)

vessels specifically designed to suit one or other purpose. In particular, I want to examine how modern potters have learnt to manipulate the existing 'vocabulary' of their craft in the search for, and development of, an individual or personal style. All the usual, as well as some less familiar, techniques are employed by the studio potter in the creation of bottle and bowl forms. But, regardless of the methods used, it can be clearly seen that the personal motivation and skill of countless individuals have provided us with a richly satisfying (and sometimes bewildering) diversity of objects within these two categories. The ability to surprise has never been the sole prerogative of the modern potter, however, for the long history of ceramics reveals many fascinating pieces challenging convention.

But what criteria are most likely to condition the potter's thinking? And to what extent do underlying principles of design or traditional practices and social or economic pressures affect the shapes of the vessels he/she makes? These are aspects that will be examined more fully in subsequent chapters.

It is never easy for a practising potter like myself to be totally objective, no matter how open-minded one's intentions or approach to the subject

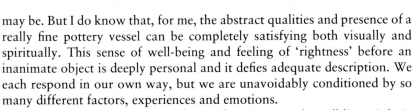

Low-fired earthenware vessel, coil-built and burnished to a high sheen. By MAGDALENE ODUNDO (UK), 1985.

'Lotus Bottle'. Coil-built in T-material with dark blue burnished slip, and red slip decorative panel, fired to 1060°C and smoked in sawdust. Height 56 cm (22 in). By JUDY TRIM (UK), 1982.
(Photo: Brian E. Rybolt)

may be. But I do know that, for me, the abstract qualities and presence of a really fine pottery vessel can be completely satisfying both visually and spiritually. This sense of well-being and feeling of 'rightness' before an inanimate object is deeply personal and it defies adequate description. We each respond in our own way, but we are unavoidably conditioned by so many different factors, experiences and emotions.

Personal preferences in vessel forms, for some people, will lie mainly in those groups which might be described as 'classical'. Perhaps strong curves and the clean, direct lines of positive, clearly defined shapes appeal to their taste above all others. It is possible to gain intense and lasting satisfaction in contemplation of these forms and of their subtle accents; but, it must also be acknowledged that the cool, reserved presence of such forms will not be equally satisfying to everyone. There are many more bold and extrovert approaches made in the design of ceramic vessels which go beyond the application of even the most riotous of patterns and brightest of colour combinations. Examples of some of the more adventurous and avant-garde pieces illustrated in this book are the results of attempts by individual potters to redefine their own concepts of bottles or bowls. Their

work is the fruit of thoughtful exploration, personal commitment, and conviction, modified to some extent by their chosen materials, methods and processes.

It is always interesting to talk with other potters about their sources of inspiration and the personal methods they have developed for dealing with problems arising in their use of materials. It seems that no other craft promotes so much discussion of techniques. Most gatherings of potters include conversations about the science as much as the art involved in their work. Both aspects are inextricably entwined and both are explored, with the generous help of potters from many parts of the world, through the pages of this book.

It is also my wish to provide the reader with a visual 'library' of shapes or profiles (see Chapter 5) in order to promote discussion of design aspects and aesthetics in tandem with the materials and processes involved in the production of studio ceramics. Too often we find the emphasis is placed in one direction at the expense of the other. Yet, in truth, all are (or ought to be) inseparable parts of the whole process and of the physical realization of the object. Of course, techniques are essential to any craft, but they should never become the dominant factor even though they may well provide the initial stimulus for a body of work. A pot which is purely a demonstration of expertise will probably appear lacking in other more intangible qualities. Equally, it is possible for good ideas to be incoherently explored through the clumsy or insensitive handling of materials. In that case, attempts are sometimes made to justify bad craftsmanship by verbally stressing the expressive content of a piece of work through some kind of explanatory title.

'Mardi Gras Nut Bowls'. Slab-built porcelain with underglaze decoration. Concave and convex plaster formers are used to support the soft clay slabs during construction and drying. Further support (with clay units, discarded later) is used while firing. 18 cm (7 in) each side. By DOROTHY HAFNER (USA), 1984. (Photo: S. Baker Vail)

'Illusion Broken Bowl'. Large serving bowl, wheel-thrown and cut by hand. Earthenware with black glaze over green slip fired to cone 02. Diameter 37 cm (14½ in). By DENISE GOYER AND ALAIN BONNEAU (Canada), 1982.

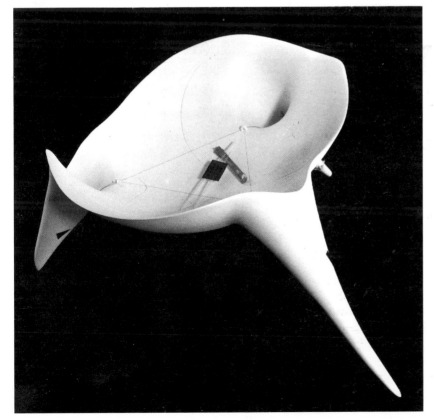

Left: 'The Poetry Stone'. Tripod bowl form constructed from porcelain, wire, bone, Plexiglass, silicon wafer fragment, and acetate. 46×23 cm (18×9 in). By ROBERTA KASERMAN (USA), 1984.

'Village Bowl'. Stoneware with oatmeal glaze. By IAN GODFREY (UK), 1978. (Photo: City Museum, Stoke-on-Trent)

Bowl, slip-cast in bone china with pierced and semi-pierced surface. Fired to 1220°C (cone 6) and finally burnished. Diameter 12 cm (4¾ in). By ANGELA VERDON (UK), 1985.

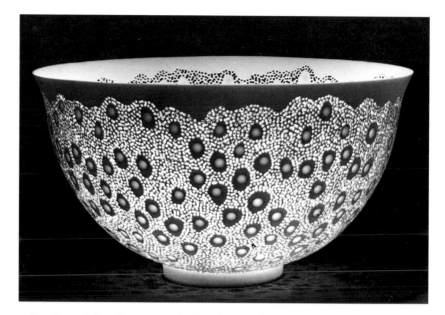

Bowls and bottles are probably the best-known, universally available, domestic containers which have been in continuous use for many centuries. They are to be found in an enormous variety of shapes and styles of decoration adapted to meet different cultural needs since pottery making first began. The bowl was probably the first form to be made in clay. It is certainly one of the most useful of all pottery vessels. Its shape has been variously adapted to suit many domestic purposes, more especially for the storage, preparation and serving of food and drink; for personal hygiene; growing plants, etc. Different social and religious practices prompted

Red earthenware moulded bowl with added red iron. By ANN HARRIS (UK). (Photo: Tim Hill)

Porcelain bowl brushed with several layers of cobalt manganese and copper slips under a barium carbonate glaze. Fired to cone 10 (1300°C) with gold and copper lustre decoration. 16.5×10 cm (6½×4 in). By MARY RICH (UK), 1985.

further developments of form and surface treatments. Modern studio potters are equally fascinated by the concept of the bowl form, which, despite continuous exploration for thousands of years, still offers enormous scope for individual interpretation and ingenuity.

A ceramic bowl is a common object found in every home whether it be used primarily for decoration, contemplation, or merely to hold a selection of fruit or salad. Bowls are wider, generally, than they are high. They are *open* forms, whose inner and outer surfaces, fully exposed to view, invite visual and tactile appreciation. Of course, all pottery vessels, especially

Stoneware bowl with wide, foliated rim, decorated with multiple slips and fired in reduction to cone 11. By JOHN GLICK (USA), 1985.

those made on the wheel, begin as open forms until the potter adjusts and adds to or subtracts from the profile of the piece growing under his/her hands. If the potter should choose to make a lid for the bowl its character and appearance will be altered, yet it remains a bowl in essence. If, on the other hand, two bowls of equal circumference are joined together rim to rim, with an opening made at the top and a neck added, the piece then becomes a bottle form which encloses, defines and occupies space in a very different way from a bowl.

We are most familiar with vessels of circular section, but both bowls and bottles lend themselves to considerable invention. Square, rectangular, oblong or oval sections are all quite common examples of symmetrical shapes, while for some potters asymmetry provides them with a more stimulating challenge.

Bottles closely rival bowls in their usefulness and popular appeal. They may be described as *closed* vessel forms whose openings are restricted in some way, although, for the purposes of this book, that does not necessarily mean that they must have a neck extension to be classified as 'bottles'. They are usually, but not always, greater in height than they are in width. Only their outer wall surface(s) can be seen and meaningfully decorated. As with all pottery vessels, any surface embellishment with pattern or texture should complement the form and enhance its sensory satisfaction. Narrow-necked bottles sometimes possess a significant feeling of tautness or tension, as if stretched almost to the point of bursting. Such forms demand to be touched, caressed.

Large, coil-built raku bottle. Diameter 56 cm (22 in), height 48 cm (19 in). By DAVID ROBERTS **(UK), 1985.**

Stoneware bottles with titanium, crystalline glazes. Height of taller piece 14 cm (5½ in). By WILLI HORNBERGER (West Germany).

Three slim vessels, hand-built with oval sections, with matt feldspathic glazes fired in reduction to cone 11. Height of tallest piece 34 cm (13½ in). By WILHELM AND ELLY KUCH (West Germany). (Photo: R. Wiech-Altdorf)

Bottle form, with precisely turned integral stopper. Thrown in stoneware with iron-spot engobe fired in reduction with later oxidation to cone 8. Height 23 cm (9 in). By THOMAS NAETHE (West Germany), 1985. (Photo: Foto Strenger)

Bottle form with integral stopper, thrown in stoneware clay with an iron-spot engobe, fired in reduction to cone 8. Height 25 cm (10 in). By THOMAS NAETHE (West Germany), 1984. (Photo: Foto Strenger)

These two basic forms, one 'open' and the other 'closed', represent the two extremes of vessel shapes. Most other vessel forms are extensions or variations falling somewhere between the two. It is those differing proportional relationships within these two 'family groups' that provide opportunities for endless study and enjoyment, while the elements of pattern, colour, tone and texture add further infinite possibilities for exploration. The choice of materials, the methods of making, and various combinations of the ceramic processes can give even more dimensions to the potter's expression. The final work will be the physical manifestation of individual feeling and understanding. Intuitive thought and action balanced by the skills born of experience all play an important part in the realization and resolution of an idea.

A certain amount of classification is possible within these two major vessel categories, based on a series of profiles which may, or may not, owe anything to functional precedent. For example, the term 'cider jar' is likely to bring to mind a particular kind of form which is basically a bottle shape. Similarly, a 'pedestal bowl' can be readily visualized, but in this case there is greater room for individual interpretation because no specific function has been ascribed to it. Historical and cultural traditions often influence our understanding, analysis, and even approval of vessel forms.

It is virtually impossible to proclaim universal ideals where matters of taste are concerned, for that is conditioned by individual perception and is

Cross-handled bottle, wood-fired stoneware. By JOHN LEACH (UK), 1983. (Photo: City Museum, Stoke-on-Trent)

Porcelain vessel with clay basket-like handle and semi-matt black, wood-ash glaze. Height 35.5 cm (14 in). By TOM COLEMAN (USA), 1985. (Photo: Rick Paulson)

bound to be limited by the breadth of one's own personal experience and degree of awareness. Fashions come and go in all things, but the underlying geometry of pottery vessels remains clear. Although many adjustments can be made to *traditional* vessel forms, such changes are rarely of a radical nature and it is more likely that it will be the colours, patterns and textures that reflect passing trends. It must be evident to all who have observed developments in contemporary studio ceramics through the 1970s and 1980s that the use of bright colours and patterns on pots marks a dramatic change from the muted tones of the previous two decades.

True inventiveness often comes from a sensitivity and understanding developed over a period of time and it usually follows concentrated thought applied to a particular idea. The hand can only move in response to orders from the brain so that action follows thought. A craft like pottery involves both mental and physical activity. It also requires the use of materials that raise a variety of problems which must be resolved if the materials are to be used successfully. It is possible to learn the basic 'rules' of any craft and, by applying a modicum of logic, most difficulties can be overcome. But, like all who work in the crafts, potters have to temper those acquired skills with discretion if their products are to become more than a sterile statement of their virtuosity.

Potting is, undoubtedly, one of the most exacting of crafts and, as previously indicated, one in which the science is essential to the art. Both must be properly understood and tackled with intuition, feeling and thought. I have found, during my thirty years of teaching, that the words 'thought' and 'thinking' tend to be associated more readily with academic disciplines like mathematics and philosophy, with scant regard being paid to the certain fact that there are different kinds of thinking. Work in all aspects of the visual arts demands a special kind of intuitive thinking that can not be purely intellectual. Knowledge can be taught, but the personal know-how, or sensitivity, needed for when and how that knowledge should be applied is an extremely important factor that distinguishes a good craftsperson from an indifferent one. Our senses are stimulated in response to experiences. Feelings emerge and grow within us to become an integral part of our lives and all that we do. Some evidence of that individual response to experience is present in all truly expressive work. The indispensable nature of this intuitive kind of thinking is, perhaps, best nurtured and developed through the practice of a craft such as pottery. A good pot is the end product of that creative thinking, supported by knowledge and executed with skill.

The way in which potters choose to present their work to the public is an important factor governing their personal image and, ultimately, the financial return they can expect to receive for their labours. Unless a potter owns a direct sales outlet, others must be found that will best complement his/her kind of work.

Selected individuals or groups are often energetically promoted by a variety of craft galleries, and there has also been a comparatively recent introduction of contemporary ceramics, including the work of living potters, into the catalogues and salerooms of well-known auction houses. This kind of exposure has created a new set of values, both monetary and aesthetic. Now that increasing numbers of people are collecting pots, for whatever motives, an overstretched supply position in the case of the most popular potters inevitably produces inflated prices which are not always a sound guide to the true artistic worth of a particular pot. The name of the maker often dictates the market price at least as much as the quality of the work. Few potters succeed in everything that they make, but a piece by a

Two porcelain bottles fired in oxidation. Heights 40 cm (15¾ in) and 13 cm (5 in). By CHRISTINE-ANN RICHARDS (UK), 1985.

Far left: Wheel-thrown bottle, porcelain with smoked terra sigillata, beige coloured with traces of metallic silver encircled by black. Height 14 cm (5½ in). By JEAN PAUL AZAIS (France), 1981. (Photo: Paul Palau)

Left: Porcelain bottle vase with tall neck. The flowing line of the profile is interrupted by slight distortion at the point where neck and shoulder meet. (This is a particular problem in porcelain when thrown vessels are constructed from two or more sections and is caused by uneven moisture content of the separate pieces, which only becomes evident in the glaze firing.) Height 30 cm (11¾ in). By GÖRGE HOHLT (West Germany).

Wheel-thrown vessel in finely grogged stoneware. Mottled white/green and black glazes. Fired in an electric kiln to cone 8. Height 28 cm (11 in). By LUCETTE GODARD (Spain), 1985. (Photo: Jorge Mauricio)

Open vessel form, porcelain with feldspathic glaze over iron-bearing slip; the rim, waist and 'skirt' provide natural boundaries for colour changes, and further emphasis is given to these by the thin bands of lighter colour that encircle the pot at those points in the profile. Ursula Scheid often uses linear accents to visualize her basic concept of a particular form. Sometimes she achieves this by using different colours or tones of slips under a glaze, and sometimes parts are left unglazed. Diameter 15.5 cm (6⅛ in).
By URSULA SCHEID (West Germany), 1985.
(Photo: Jochen Schade)

'named' potter will usually command a higher price than a superior pot by one who is little known. However, it is notable also that many collectors now regularly and enthusiastically attend student exhibitions at colleges around Britain and elsewhere, prepared to pay high prices for pieces by potters who have yet to establish themselves.

We live in an age of 'personalities'. The anonymity so cherished by writers like the Japanese Soetsu Yanagi (*The Unknown Craftsman*) appeals to very few of today's potters. A signature or stamp on a piece is usually appreciated, and often expected, by the purchaser and that mark also serves as an advertisement for the maker. I know of several potters who, having made a piece which for some reason does not match up to the standards they set for themselves (yet is considered too good to discard), painstakingly grind down their signature until it is completely removed. The pot is then sold as a 'second' and, although still possessing the potter's unmistakable identity, no longer has his/her approval as a top-quality piece.

Of course, professional potters must take market forces into account if they are to satisfy their need to survive by selling the products of their workshops, but to make those forces the prime conditioner for the work would be, almost certainly, far too restrictive. However, they can, and should, pursue their ideals with dedication and conviction if they are to create a genuine market demand for their work that is based upon consistent quality with at least a touch of originality.

In the absence of a definitive set of rules that we can conveniently apply in judgement of contemporary ceramics we can, of course, take the line of least resistance and accept what others may tell us. But we are all of us different and should exercise the freedom we have to make up our own minds. How dull life would be if we all thought the same thoughts and felt and reacted to experiences in the same way! Living together would probably be simpler, but we do seem to need the constant stimulus of conflict and controversy in order to develop. We have to decide for ourselves what we like and admire, and why we do so. There is no room for dogma in ceramics because there has never been one 'correct' way of working with clay. Even so, there will always be those who attempt to denigrate work which does not fit within any recognizable category that they can easily define, or does not coincide with their taste of the moment.

It has become fashionable of late to kick against the Anglo-Oriental aestheticism propounded by Bernard Leach. Some have gone further and accused Leach of blighting successive generations with his particular brand

Wheel-thrown bowl, altered while still wet, painted with white slip and overlapping matt white and clear glazes, reduction-fired to cone 10. Diameter 44 cm (17¼ in).
By NEIL MOSS (USA), 1985.
(Photo: Brian Goodman)

Porcelain bowl with celadon glaze, cobalt and iron banding, and spots with incised diagonal steps. Fired in reduction to cone 10 (1300°C). Diameter 12 cm (4¾ in). By DEREK CLARKSON (UK), 1985.

Below: 'Zig-zag Green'. Porcelain bowl in neriage technique, fired to cone 10. Diameter 21 cm (8¼ in). By HANS MUNCK ANDERSEN (Denmark), 1985. (Photo: Wolf Böwig)

of philosophy. Nevertheless, Leach and his immediate followers achieved a level of recognition and public acceptance from which all potters subsequently have benefited. It is natural and inevitable that guidelines laid down by others should be challenged. This creates room for new ideas and fresh opportunities to work in any way that best suits personal concepts and situations. However, such freedom can generate its own problems. The greatest of these concern standards and the question of focus. Apart from subjective feelings, how can we best evaluate the work? What do we measure it against? Should we rely on some kind of consensus?

My experience over many years of assessing the ceramics of college and university students and in selecting pots for exhibitions in Britain and elsewhere suggests that nothing can be absolute because the subjective element is always present in the visual arts, as it is in any other field of human expression. Individuals within a group will argue for their beliefs but, ultimately, they will tend to gravitate in their assessment towards a supportable norm, subordinating their stronger preferences in the interests of agreement. Changing the composition of the group brings different feelings and ideals into the discussion and the findings may differ also.

It is much easier to evaluate the qualities of craftsmanship, the degree of skill exhibited through the handling of materials and processes, than it is to agree on evidence of feeling, emotional content, or expressive elements communicated through a piece of pottery. I remember reading a national newspaper review of the Hans Coper retrospective exhibition held in the Sainsbury Centre for the Visual Arts at the University of East Anglia, Norwich, England, in 1983, which described his pots as 'dull and lacking variety in shape and colour, being mainly black and white'. I had just written a piece on the same exhibition for the *UEA Newsletter*, in which I enthused over Coper's dedicated exploration of vessel forms and the many, subtle variations he had developed. There was plenty of colour, too, for anyone who really cared to look. That exhibition was, for me, a deeply moving experience and I spent a good deal of time there among those pots, alone and with my students, seeing something fresh on each occasion.

It is not always possible to visit all the exhibitions one would like to and, without the physical presence of the actual object for reference, we often have to accept two-dimensional images to stimulate our consciousness. Photographs are poor substitutes for reality but they do provide us with readily accessible images that should be stimulating and satisfying in themselves. We should use them as surrogates to broaden our knowledge and increase our understanding and awareness. We can still accept, reject or question their value or that of the objects they represent. They may help us to confirm or deny previously held notions and concepts, and by so doing we respond and are forced to think.

As a practising potter myself, whose work consists largely of bowls of one sort or another and whose second preference is for the making of bottles, I often discover fresh inspiration from seeing all kinds of pots in museums and in commercial galleries. Such visual stimulus may result in no immediate developments, but the experience usually contributes to my understanding and appreciation of the form and surface of ceramic vessels. I would not wish to forego any opportunity to study ceramics in this way, but I have often wished that I might also have some more permanent, readily available source of reference at home. It is my hope that the material gathered together in this book will serve as sustenance for all involved or interested in ceramics at any level, for I have no doubt that ceramic vessels in the form of bowls and bottles will continue to be made, used, enjoyed and appreciated as long as potters and clay exist.

Opposite: **Porcelain vessel with carved relief decoration under a semi-matt glaze, white shading to pink where held by the carving. Fired in reduction to 1360°C. 18 × 19.5 × 6.5 cm (7 × 7¾ × 2⅝ in). By** KARL SCHEID **(West Germany), 1986. (Photo: Jochen Schade)**

Bottle vase, stoneware, with a counterchange pattern where the matt black glaze has been resisted. Height 20 cm (8 in). By HILDEGARD EGGEMANN **(West Germany), 1984.**

2. VESSEL FORM

I believe that form should be the prime concern of the potter. He/she may well create pieces to carry a particular kind of decoration but, at best, that decoration can only complement the form and enhance its appeal.

The form of a vessel often suggests that it can perform some kind of useful purpose in addition to the decorative aspect of its being. When vessels are primarily intended to serve as containers, that special function must be carefully considered and incorporated into the initial design. A bowl which is likely to be carried or moved around frequently may need to be given handles or lugs, and the placement of those additions has to take into account the weight and balance of the vessel when full as well as when empty. Any additions will also affect the visual balance; they may become dominant features that attract attention to those parts of the form to which they are attached. A Greek kylix, for example, has handles which can appear almost like wings, with an upward movement that extends the form out into the surrounding space. Occasionally, in fact, potters apply false lugs or handles solely for extra visual interest.

Potters have to learn how best to handle their materials and to control the chemistry involved before they are able to work with any real fluency. There are so many facets to that chemistry that it can prove daunting. Most potters, therefore, tend to confine themselves to areas which experience has proven to suit their style of work. Once they have mastered the science and technology, however, they must then endeavour to apply them in a skilful, yet personal and expressive manner. If they also have a genuine and deeply felt love of clay (and many would indeed claim this affinity

Greek kylix, 520 BC.

Batter bowl made in a grey, stoneware clay with a feldspathic glaze containing 1 per cent red iron oxide and 5 per cent rutile. A splash of an iron/rutile slip has also been applied, with a very large brush, to increase the textural appearance of the glaze surface. The pulled handle has been attached to the rim so that it has become a natural, flowing extension of it. The functional and aesthetic aspects have been happily married together in this piece: it pours well and looks fine whether empty or full. Diameter 19 cm ($7\frac{1}{2}$ in). By RICK SHERMAN (USA), 1986. (Photo: Sharon Devaux)

Opposite: Tall stoneware vessel in the form of a basket, wheel-thrown and then squeezed into an oval section at the rim, with a matt, wood-ash glaze fired in reduction. Height 51 cm (20 in). By PATRICK HORSLEY (USA), 1986. (Photo: Bill Backuber)

Above: Salt-glazed stoneware bowl, fumed with ferric chloride. Fired to cone 10. Diameter 30 cm (11¾ in). By JANET MANSFIELD (**Australia**), 1985.

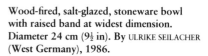

Wood-fired, salt-glazed, stoneware bowl with raised band at widest dimension. Diameter 24 cm (9½ in). By ULRIKE SEILACHER (**West Germany**), 1986.

Pot with scalloped edge, hand-built, with painted slip decoration. By ELIZABETH FRITSCH (**UK**), 1974. (Photo: Crafts Council)

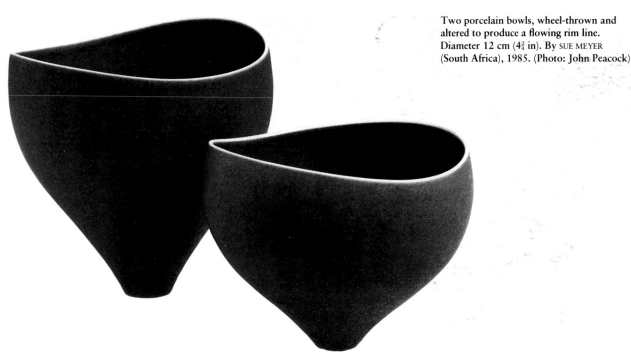

Two porcelain bowls, wheel-thrown and altered to produce a flowing rim line. Diameter 12 cm (4¾ in). By SUE MEYER (South Africa), 1985. (Photo: John Peacock)

with their chosen material), that feeling will, usually, be transmitted through their work. Equally important is the manipulation of certain basic elements of design used to create a kind of visual vocabulary, consciously or otherwise, by which physical substance is given to their ideas and feelings. A good potter is able to exploit contrasts such as light and dark, thick and thin, fast and slow, rough and smooth, pattern and plain, etc., in order to arrive at some kind of balance and harmony of form and surface.

Bowls

Bowls in one form or another have been in use constantly for many thousands of years. At first animal skins, seashells and seed casings served (and still serve in some situations) as ready-made containers for food and drink, but since the discovery that clay could be easily fashioned, and then hardened by fire, opportunities have been taken to create an enormous variety of ceramic vessels either to serve some specific function or to exist in their own right as art objects. Today, in addition to the traditional materials such as clay, wood, glass, metal and leather, modern technology has provided us with plastics which can assume almost any shape or form. These are relatively cheap, serviceable, and available in many different colours and textures. They do undoubtedly have an attraction of their own, but they also have a somewhat cold presence lacking in life and liveliness. Given the option of a plastic or a ceramic fruit bowl for use and display in the home, very few people would be likely to choose one in the former material.

A bowl is potentially the most satisfying of all pottery forms both to make and to own. Of course, there are good and bad examples, as in everything, but the best are timeless in their appeal. As useful objects they have many varied applications which have been developed over thousands of years. They are forms which offer containment and protection in an open manner. The observer is not normally excluded from the interior of a bowl and can gain pleasure from all its surfaces. One can physically feel its

'Fascinating Rhythm'. Hand-built porcelain bowl made from inlaid coloured sheets, unglazed. Graded colours have been assembled vertically, rather like thin slices of agate, to create a positive yet delicate pattern. Diameter 18 cm (7 in). By CURTIS AND SUZAN BENZLE (USA), 1985.

'Groove Bowl'. Large serving bowl, wheel-thrown in earthenware clay with black glaze fired to cone 02. Diameter 37 cm (14½ in). By DENISE GOYER AND ALAIN BONNEAU (Canada), 1978.

thickness and judge its weight in relation to its size and capacity, and when a bowl can be held comfortably in cupped hands it offers a natural communion that should provide tactile, as well as visual, satisfaction.

The main elements determining the form and character of an open pottery vessel are the foot; the length and directional changes of profile; and the rim, lip, or final 'horizon line'. Surface treatments merely modify that form through the incorporation of pattern, texture or colour. The permutations therein are truly infinite. Simple forms, with few positive changes of direction in the profile, are capable of supporting quite complex patterns and this is an aspect that is illustrated more fully in subsequent chapters.

We have already defined a bowl as an open vessel which is usually wider than it is high and whose inner and outer surfaces are both offered to view. Ceramics, like plastics, can take virtually any form, colour, texture and decorative treatment. In general, the external profile (or silhouette) of a bowl provides us with the necessary visual clues as to its character and function (if any be intended). Apart from any consideration of use or purpose in hand-made pots, however, we are concerned also with the expression and communication of human feeling, because pottery produced by hand always reflects something of the individual who made it.

Clay is one of the most responsive materials in common use and the processes of the ceramic medium can be orchestrated, as well as manipulated, by a skilled and sensitive potter. For example, elegance can be expressed in a bowl by making it spring from a small foot; similarly, strength, solidity and stability can be imparted in another given a broader base. Much will depend on the direction and continuity of the profile line and the angle and speed of its ascent from foot to rim. The main body of the vessel may also be elevated upon a foot-ring or pedestal, and the use of such a device will often enhance that image of elegance if the profile line is more generous than that of a static cylinder. A pedestal with a flowing line that tapers inwards before curving out to cup and merge into a swelling bowl form contributes much to a feeling of gentle tranquillity, echoing familiar growth forms found in nature. Round bowls, with a small base or foot in relation to the main body of the piece, have a strong attraction for many people, especially when the form curves upwards and out like an opening flower bud.

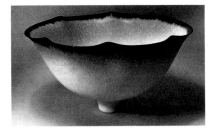

Porcelain bowl, thrown, with barium and zinc cream glazes. Brushed with copper and fired in oxidation at 1280°C. Diameter 25 cm (10 in). By RAY SILVERMAN (UK).

Above: Porcelain bowl, with painted black porcelain slip and textured exterior, unglazed, reduction-fired in a gas kiln to cone 9. Diameter 20 cm (8 in). By HORST GÖBBELS (West Germany).
(Photo: Willi Faahsen)

Stoneware bowl made from two thrown pots, stained black with blue lustre.
By ALAN BARRATT-DANES (UK), 1984.
(Photo: City Museum, Stoke-on-Trent)

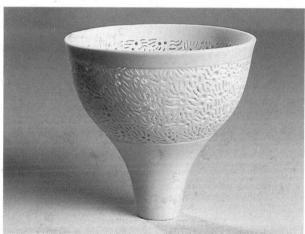

Making processes and design considerations

The potter's wheel offers a quick and easy method of producing vessels in clay and the centrifugal force developed by the rotating wheel-head aids the production of open forms. The vast majority of bowls throughout the long history of ceramics have been circular in plan. Many more wheel-thrown pieces have been altered away from the round by beating, stretching, pinching, carving or faceting at a later stage, and some of them may have additions which help to disguise their circular origin. But the round form evolved naturally and undoubtedly it has a greater physical strength. It possesses a sense of completeness. It is pleasant to handle and it is better able to withstand knocks that would shatter a rectangular, flat-sided form, because the shock wave is dissipated over a wider area. For the same reason it is also safer to apply pressure from the outside inwards when carving a round, unfired, leather-hard bowl. The reverse process requires extremely careful support of the wall at the point of pressure because the stress tends to be localized over a tiny area.

Top: Porcelain bowl with textured outer surface produced by carving with a wire loop tool when leather-hard. Diameter 30.5 cm (12 in). By PETER LANE (UK), 1986. (Photo: Peter Lane)

Above left: Slip-cast vessel, pierced and polished (unglazed), fired to cone 7 in oxidation. Diameter 8.5 cm (3⅜ in). By SANDRA BLACK (Australia), 1985. (Photo: Paul Finlay)

Above right: A simple thrown bowl, very functional with its smooth interior and broad base. The profile is given some interest by the rippled upper section where the throwing rings break through the tenmoku glaze. Fired to cone 10 in reduction. Diameter 27 cm (10½ in). By JAN SCHACHTER (USA), 1985. (Photo: Robert Aude)

Open disc-shaped vessel elevated on a tall foot. The surface is textured by melt fissures and fire marks. Dimensions of the top 24.5×9 cm (9⅝×3½ in). **By** OTTO NATZLER (USA), 1984.
(Photo: Gail Reynolds Natzler)

There are other functional factors in favour of a vessel with a continuous inner curve. Apart from the obvious hygienic advantages, hands, spoons and ladles work more efficiently where there are no inside corners. A rounded bottom can serve the need for stability better than a flat base, foot-ring or legs, which would be essential for a level one if the bowl is to stand on an uneven surface such as an earth floor. This can be observed in many pots hand-built in underdeveloped countries, particularly in parts of Africa and Central or South America.

A bowl without a foot-ring or other means of raising it up is unlikely to convey a feeling of elegance so much as a kind of solid dependability, unless the area of contact between its base and the surface upon which it sits is tiny in relation to the bowl's height and width. The size of any raised foot, and whether it is vertical or slopes inwards or outwards, has a critical bearing not only on the visual and practical stability of the vessel but also on its character. The way in which the foot joins the bottom of the bowl is equally important. It may be with a positive change of direction and might

Porcelain bowl with carved design around the rim under a celadon glaze. Diameter 13 cm (5 in). By SCOTT MALCOLM (USA), 1985.

even be given greater emphasis in some way; or it may flow into the bowl so that it appears as a fully integrated, natural development of the form.

Most of the foregoing observations refer to bowls of circular section, but the same principles can also be applied to other symmetrical forms having square, rectangular or oval sections. The problems and possibilities arising in asymmetric pieces will be examined later.

The treatment of the top edge, or rim, and its relationship to the form it terminates, affects the character of the bowl almost as much as does the foot. A thick or ledged rim which might be complementary and particularly suited to a stoneware bowl will, almost certainly, appear out

Two vessels with bevelled rims and lustred interiors. Diameter of shallow bowl 32 cm (12½ in). By NURIA PIE BARRUFET (Spain), 1986.

Porcelain bowl, thrown with a flattened rim which was then inlaid with stained porcelain. The exterior is polished after the final firing; the inside is glazed. Height 18 cm (7 in). By GABRIELE KLANN (West Germany), 1986.

Stoneware bowl with ledged rim and iron spots breaking through the glaze, reduction-fired to cone 10. Diameter 22 cm (8⅝ in). By VOLKER ELLWANGER (West Germany), 1984.

of place as the final statement of one made in fine porcelain. Earthenware and stoneware clays have a fairly granular composition which is often strengthened by compressing and thickening the top edges of pots at the throwing stage, making them more resistant to chipping in use. Porcelain, on the other hand, is a comparatively dense material whose fine texture encourages the potter to make thin rims that enhance the delicacy of the piece without the same degree of risk to its durability. With a wide, shallow bowl the thickness of the rim assumes greater importance, since we are more likely to look down on it and into the bowl rather than to contemplate the external profile. A taller piece demands our attention in a different way.

Opposite above: Four bowls, thrown and altered, with added handles extending outwards from the rims. Coloured slips resisted and overlaid under a salt glaze produce rich colours and strong patterns and textures. Each diameter 27 cm (10½ in). By SUZY ATKINS (France), 1986. (Photo: Pierre Soissons)

Porcelain cup inlaid with a design depicting a magpie. The colours are blue, cream, white, black and brown. Fired in reduction to cone 6. Height 10 cm (4 in). By SONY MANNING (**Australia**), 1985.

Opposite below: Stoneware bowl, reduction-fired to cone 6A, with unglazed areas, feldspathic glaze, engobes and cobalt colorants. Diameter 41 cm (16 in). By THOMAS NAETHE (West Germany), 1986. (Photo: Foto Strenger)

Thrown porcelain bowl, squeezed into an oval shape at the top and inlaid with coloured clay on one side only. Height 13 cm (5 in). By GABRIELE KLANN (West Germany), 1986.

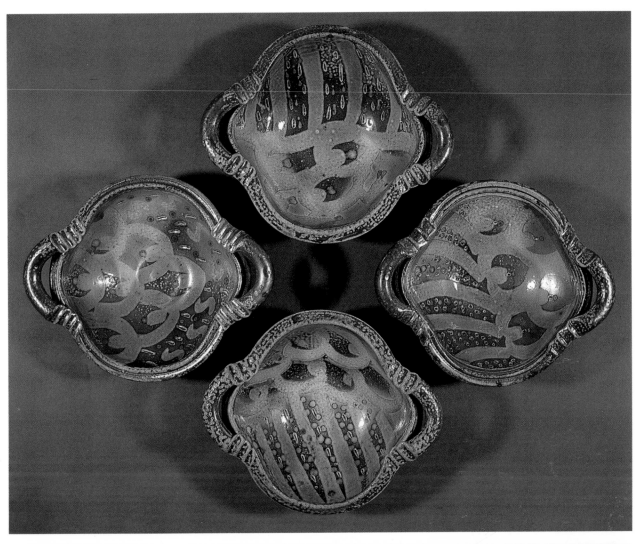

Hand-built stoneware bowl with green bands under matt white glaze, fired in an electric kiln to Orton cone 8. Diameter 26 cm (10¼ in). By JOHN WARD (UK).

When a bowl has perpendicular walls, high in proportion to its diameter, the inner surface is less obvious. The visual interest of the piece will then depend upon the way in which the exterior surface treatment complements the form. For example, the simple application on a bowl of contrasting vertical or horizontal stripes alone can heighten an illusion of dimension or volume, in the same way that certain vertical linear designs on textile fabrics can be used to disguise a portly human figure.

Certain thrown shapes, which evolved from the need to store foods and liquids, have their origins way back in history. Most are familiar and

Stoneware bowl, wheel-thrown, with red-brown slip and wax-resist decoration under satin-matt, black, feldspathic glaze. Diameter 23 cm (9 in). By WERNER NOWKA (West Germany), 1984.

instantly recognizable. Others can be identified with particular regions of the world by virtue of their shape, volume, size and proportions, and especially by their style of decoration. It is possible to find infinite variations in the profiles alone. Many of these subtle differences can be found within any apparently simple category. All containers must have a floor, and walls of some sort sufficiently high and broad to support, protect and hold the contents safely. It would seem, therefore, that nothing could be more straightforward for a potter with a wheel than opening out the centre of a spinning ball of clay and drawing the fingers outwards, gathering a thick circle of the material to pull up into a wall. The action is simple enough in itself, but those movements must be sensitively directed and the pressure of the fingers controlled in order to create the form required.

Wheel-thrown bowls develop naturally in the sense that the centrifugal force of the revolving wheel contributes to the sideways extension of the spinning clay. The potter has to co-ordinate the speed of rotation with the upward pressure of his/her hands. The wider the piece becomes, the more slowly the wheel should rotate if the potter is to retain control of the bowl's profile. A wide diameter at the rim over a relatively narrow foot will require that sufficient thickness be retained at the base and in the lower walls to prevent collapse at this stage. Excess material is easily removed later when the leather-hard bowl is inverted, recentred on the wheel and trimmed. Particular attention must be paid to the inner profile when throwing because, where the wall is to be of even thickness, this will determine the final form. A fluent thrower will sense the changing capacity of the clay body to support its own weight as the work proceeds. The wetter the developing pot becomes, the greater the risk of collapse, so the need for smooth lubrication must be balanced by an intuitive assessment of the condition of the clay.

Individual potters come to terms with their particular limitations and have to discover their own methods best suited to forming the shapes they wish to make. Some will use throwing ribs to aid the curvature and

Wheel-thrown bowl, burnished and wood-fired in reduction. Diameter 48 cm (19 in). By PETRUS SPRONK (**Australia**), 1985. (Photo: Michael Kluvanek)

Porcelain bowl, thrown and inlaid with coloured clays. The interior is glazed with a transparent feldspathic glaze, but the outside is unglazed and polished smooth. Fired in an electric kiln to cone 8. Diameter 16 cm (6¼ in). By GABRIELE KLANN (West Germany), 1986.

stretching of the clay while it rotates on the wheel. Others will prefer to rely on immediate, direct contact through the use of their fingers alone. The choice is a personal one, but the tools and methods employed, whatever they may be, will all contribute something to the final character of the work.

Most of my own work is in porcelain, which, for me, implies purity, delicacy (usually aided by translucency), elegance and a sharp clarity of profile. The first of these requirements is sought not only through the use of clean materials, tools and working environment but also in the initial concept of both form and surface. The suggestion of elegance in a piece often arises as a direct result of one's approach to that concept and the attempt at its resolution. It is a process of feeling, thought and action inextricably bound up together. The clay must be in good condition – neither too hard nor too soft – for throwing the shape one has in mind; but, above all, one's mental attitude must be attuned and committed to the work. I must confess to suffering occasional periods of intense frustration when either or both these conditions are not fully met. At such times one has the option of postponing the work or persevering, sometimes for several days, until one breaks through what I like to refer to as the 'pain barrier' and the work begins to flow with less conscious effort.

I work mainly on the wheel because it provides me with a quick and efficient means of exploring circular bowl forms. Even within the limitation of the circular plan there is plenty of scope for individual expression. Porcelain is particularly smooth and sensuous to work on the wheel. Opening the clay and pulling it up and out to form a bowl can be an especially satisfying activity when the clay stretches creamily between fingers that are pressing, caressing and coaxing it towards the shape perceived by one's inner eye.

If translucency and refinement are among my aims I often prefer to eliminate the more vigorous marks of the making process. Throwing rings in porcelain, for example, can be a disruptive feature, underlying and interfering with any subsequent surface decoration. Flexible, kidney-

Porcelain bowl, wheel-thrown and inlaid with different greys and light blue coloured porcelain, reduction-fired to cone 13. Diameter 24.5 cm (9⅝ in). By RAINER DOSS (West Germany), 1986. (Photo: Antje Doss)

Porcelain bowl, wheel-thrown and carved under a satin-matt, white glaze. Oxidized to cone 9. Diameter approximately 13 cm (5 in). By PETER LANE (UK), 1985.

Porcelain bowl, thrown and altered at the rim while still wet. The flowing linear pattern was incised at the leather-hard stage. By KEN CATBAGAN (USA), 1985.

shaped steel ribs, therefore, are among my favourite tools. These are thin enough to provide an almost natural extension of the fingers, for they can be flexed to fit most contours of the inner and outer walls as the bowl develops. Their use smoothes the surface of the clay, removing throwing ridges (although some slight evidence of these may return in the final firing of porcelain). Another advantage offered by sensitive throwing ribs is that they present a broader and more even pressure to the thinning wall, reducing the ever-present risk involved when fingers start drying and sticking to the clay, a situation which can cause sudden distortion. Should a wide bowl form be snagged by unlubricated fingers it will probably be lost. The rib, on the other hand, allows the potter to work with far less water and to clean any excess slip from the surface of the bowl at the same time. The extravagant use of water or the accumulation of too much surface slip during throwing can weaken the body and lead to its collapse.

My own bowls often begin life on the wheel as thick-bottomed cylinders. These are then stretched with the flexible steel rib. Starting at the rim and making use of the centrifugal force of the rotating wheel, gentle pressure is applied on the inner surface, as the hand moves down towards the centre. That pressure is directed downwards along and through the vertical length of the wall, rather than outwards. It can be controlled in an uninterrupted curve of virtually any radius or, by varying the degree and point of pressure, a central well can be created, from above which the bowl springs out and upwards quite dramatically. The outer profile is ultimately trimmed away from the initial thickness left in the base in order to complement and reflect the inner shape. Even so, the final form must be clearly understood and anticipated during the throwing stage because no amount of trimming will resurrect a weakly conceived form.

Throwing can also be the starting point for forms which are later to be manipulated away from the circular plan. There are many different possibilities. One of the most common is to cut a pointed, oval-shaped piece out of the base and then push together and rejoin the cut edges. In the process the rim also becomes radically altered and can either be left or cut

Stoneware bowl with faceted walls and tenmoku glaze. Diameter 16 cm (6¼ in). By HORST KERSTAN (West Germany), 1985. (Photo: Landesgewerbeamt)

Burnished bowl with three shards fired in oxidation. The main body of the bowl was fired separately in reduction. One shard is decorated with a painted pattern and the others with some smoke work. The potter sometimes breaks pieces, fires them separately and glues them together later, before finishing the pot 'with gold-leaf work which I learnt from a Greek icon painter'. Diameter 18 cm (7 in). By PETRUS SPRONK (Australia), 1985. (Photo: Michael Kluvanek)

Double-walled raku bowl thrown in one piece using the 'trapped air technique', with hand-built additions. The whole piece, including the combed texture, is completed in the wet state on the wheel. The base is trimmed when leather-hard. Colour comes from copper carbonate with barium carbonate and manganese dioxide. Bisqued at 900°C (Orton cone 011) and refired to 1100°C (Orton cone 03) with post-firing reduction. The basically simple profile of this bowl appears to be tautly held by encircling bands tensioned by the four wedges. The form, with its additions, is reminiscent of certain ritualistic vessels of ancient times. Diameter 38 cm (15 in). By JEFF MINCHAM (Australia), 1986. (Photo: Grant Hancock)

Porcelain bowl with incised geometric pattern covered with a slip glaze composed of seven parts manganese dioxide, one part copper oxide, and three parts red earthenware clay (all by volume). This produces a dark, rich metallic surface in gold and black when fired in oxidation to cone 8. Other mixtures of copper, manganese and clay can also be used to obtain a similar metallic gold, but this should be used with discretion, not least because the heavy concentration of oxides causes the slip to run down onto the kiln shelves when too thickly applied or when overfired. By PETER BEARD (UK), 1985. (Photo: John Wylie)

down to form another horizon line. A certain amount of reshaping can be done immediately after throwing, but such treatment is usually reserved for bowls which require little or no further trimming. While the clay is still wet the rim can be pulled into an oval or rectangular line with the fingers. As the clay stiffens in drying it can be tackled more vigorously. One popular method for wide-based bowls is that of beating the walls with a wooden paddle to make faceted sides and a square opening at the top.

When leather-hard a thrown bowl can be cut in various ways and rejoined to create a new shape; or pieces can be added to extend the height or width of the rim. A foot can also be added or altered to elevate the form, or increase the height, or improve stability. A whole host of additions and subtractions affecting the appearance and character of forms and surfaces can be employed at different stages. These will be discussed in more detail later in this chapter. Some potters are even known to break a bisque-fired bowl, to refire the pieces separately with different glazes (at the same temperature to equalize the shrinking of the body) and then to reassemble the pot using a strong adhesive.

However, the most basic open vessel or bowl one could choose to make on the wheel would have a flat bottom where, on opening up the spinning clay, the fingers have moved outwards parallel to the horizontal wheel-head. Its wall would be vertical and probably no higher than its radial dimension. Such a piece would be very stable and would sit firmly on a flat surface; but it is likely to be an unremarkable and uninspiring form aesthetically, unless some kind of pattern or decorative treatment is added. The simple forms of many seventeenth-century posset pots, for example, are merely cylindrical vessels to which two or more handles have been attached; yet freely applied slip-trailed patterns under a warm, honey-coloured, lead glaze give these basic open vessels life and a particular character of their own.

Cylindrical posset pot, buff earthenware clay decorated with brown and buff slips. The inscription reads: 'The Best Is Not Too Good For You 1725'. Made in Staffordshire. (Photo: City Museum, Stoke-on-Trent)

Cylindrical bowl, porcelain, partly
decorated with iron slip and partly
unglazed. Fired in reduction to 1360°C.
Diameter 13 cm (5 in). By URSULA SCHEID
(West Germany), 1982.
(Photo: Bernd P. Göbbels)

Opposite above: Stoneware bowl with
incised, linear, geometric design. Diameter
approximately 30.5 cm (12 in). By CHRIS
JENKINS (UK), 1984.

Right: Porcelain bowl, thrown and turned,
with celadon glaze and kaki spots over
incised decoration. Fired in reduction to
cone 10 (1300°C). Diameter 8 cm (3 in).
By DEREK CLARKSON (UK), 1985.
(Photo: David Seed)

Opposite below: Stoneware bowl,
wheel-thrown and altered with clay
additions. The richly coloured and textured
surface was produced with an alumina matt
glaze containing charcoal briquet ash and
reduction-fired to cone 10. Diameter 44 cm
(17¼ in). By NEIL MOSS (USA), 1985.
(Photo: Brian Goodman)

Cylindrical porcelain bowl with mottled
zinc barium glaze. Fired in oxidation to
cone 9 (1280°C). Diameter 20 cm (8 in).
By RAY SILVERMAN (UK), 1985.

Individual explorations of form

Some examples of ways in which contemporary potters have created extra
visual interest in shallow, cylindrical bowls are illustrated here in the work
of **Ray Silverman, Neil Moss, Ursula Scheid, Derek Clarkson** and **Chris
Jenkins.**

Ray Silverman (UK) has softened and indented the rim of his
straight-sided porcelain bowl and given the top edge stronger emphasis by
darkening it with oxides. The glazed sides are speckled with more of the
same colour to enliven the surface. Indentations in the rim of the bowl by
Neil Moss (USA) mark the points at which small pellets of clay have been
attached and smoothed down to give it a distinctive identity. The ash glaze
has run down the wall accentuating its verticality.

The bowl by **Ursula Scheid** (West Germany) is clinically precise. A small
foot raises it up slightly, leaving the bottom edge of the wall sharply
defined. The fractional curvature of the wall is inward, away from the
vertical, so that the unglazed bands which tightly encircle the pot appear to
be holding it under compression. A thin, dark line runs around the inside
and briefly eases the transition from light to dark. **Derek Clarkson**'s (UK)
bowl has a taller, more noticeable foot, but an equally sharp bottom edge
to the wall. The tension is maintained by the slight inward taper towards
the rim, which then completes the wall with an outward flourish. The bowl
by **Chris Jenkins** (UK) also curves inward but only at the top, making it
convex in contrast to the concave movement seen in the previous two
examples. The incised linear pattern divides the wall horizontally into two
equal parts, while a further division by vertical lines produces adjoining
squares. These squares are themselves subdivided by alternating
arrangements of vertical, horizontal and diagonal lines: a deliberate
exercise in geometric design.

Porcelain bowl with carved rim design of hills and trees. White dolomite glaze with airbrushed copper carbonate shading at the top. Fired to cone 9 in an electric kiln. Diameter 19 cm (7½ in). By PETER LANE (UK), 1981.

If, however, the potter describes an upward curve inside with the fingertips while opening the ball of clay, the options are multiplied considerably. The form itself will allow room for much more individual expression because the soft clay responds to the slightest changes in pressure. An uninterrupted curving profile may have its greatest width at any point, but it is usually most effective when placed above or below the centre. An interesting exercise is to make several variations of the same bowl by adjusting the position of the widest part. Even very subtle differences will materially affect the character and appeal of each bowl and this is most evident when they are all placed side by side in a line in order to view the profiles. The acceptability and success, or otherwise, of any simple piece approached in this way are mainly dependent upon its proportional relationships. My experience in potting and teaching suggests that most people will agree on the selection of one particular piece from among a group of similar pots, although it is often difficult to pinpoint exactly why it should give them greater satisfaction than others within the same family of forms.

Where practical domestic requirements have to be considered as an essential part of the design, traditional precedents are likely to exert a strong influence on the form if not the decoration of a vessel. This is because the most suitable and successful forms for most domestic vessels evolved to fulfil specific needs. They were developed further and refined through constant use over many centuries. Differences in profile of wheel-thrown vessels intended for everyday use, therefore, tend to be slight. Subtle variations in these traditional shapes are due as much to individual interpretation as to any change in their domestic purpose.

The major interest of contemporary pots designed for daily use, especially for serving food, is often focused upon their surface treatment in colour, texture or pattern. There is a current fashion for bright colours in pottery, as well as in clothes and furnishings, which has released the wares

Slip-cast and carved porcelain bowl fired to cone 7 in oxidation. Diameter 10.5 cm (4⅛ in). By SANDRA BLACK (Australia), 1985. (Photo: John Austin)

of an increasing number of 'domestic' potters from the anonymity of those ubiquitous brown, black and oatmeal glazes. Whether this latest explosion of decorative wares, or the more bizarre deviations of vessel form, will survive to become a respected part of our ceramic tradition is a debatable issue, but it is fun while it lasts. Although, sadly, there can be few truly innovative people, there are many others who do possess the ability to work in an individual way and who can explore changing ideas and reflect social trends that place their work in context of both time and place.

I have already pointed out the importance of the top edge of a pot. It may terminate the form completely at the throwing stage but it may also be prepared for further treatment later. Altering the rims of bowls by cutting away or adding clay can radically change the appearance of even the most orthodox bowl shapes. Carving the rims of porcelain bowls into flowing curves and peaks to suggest landscape horizons has been a particular interest of mine for several years.

The 'plan' of a round bowl is immediately adjusted when parts of the top edge are removed. This must be borne in mind and related to the new rim or 'horizon line' for both aesthetic and physical reasons. Deep cuts made in the rim of a thinly potted porcelain bowl, for example, will cause it to distort to a greater or lesser degree, according to the number, shape and placement of cuts, when fired to maturation. However, the potter can control, and certainly reduce, deformation by carefully balancing the design with a view to symmetry. When pieces are cut away from two opposing points on the rim of a finely thrown porcelain bowl these sections will be drawn closer together during the firing, while the uncut perimeter will bow outwards. This produces a quite attractive oval plan. Quartering the rim by making cuts at four equidistant points tends to give the form a rather static feeling. Three regularly placed cuts (even when subdivided further into six), on the other hand, usually produce a flowing movement more in sympathy with the circularity of the bowl.

Hand-built stoneware bowl with oxides under a matt white glaze fired in an electric kiln to Orton cone 8. The wall has been cut and the top edge reshaped, suggesting overlapping petal forms. Diameter 31 cm (12¼ in). By JOHN WARD (UK).

Single cuts at the rim are more noticeable and often disturbing to look at because they interrupt the geometry with uncompromising suddenness. This can create a somewhat uncomfortable feeling, as illustrated by the work of **Stephanie De Lange** (USA). Her slip-cast bowls take the form of a perfect half sphere, with an equally positive cylindrical foot. These pieces have a hard, machined, almost metallic appearance, which is accentuated by the nature of the clipped cuts made with pinking shears while the clay was still leather-hard. Both high- and low-fired glazes were used, changing from one to the other at the cut line. She says of these pieces that she began 'pushing the pottery towards sculpture' in 1978 by cutting the rims of bowls and cylinders with pinking shears: 'I wanted metaphorically and literally to open up the pottery and give it a twist.'

'Fragments of Bottles'. Wheel-thrown porcelain vessels. The white piece is porcelain-fired to cone 9, and the black piece is made from a stoneware body fired with sodium carbonate to cone 1. Height of taller vessel approximately 32 cm (12½ in). By HORST GÖBBELS (West Germany). (Photo: Seyok)

Porcelain bottles and clipped porcelain bowls. The potter explains: 'The bodies of the bottles and bowls and their necks and feet are slip-cast separately, trimmed and assembled. The rims of the bowls were then softened and cut with pinking shears. The parts of the bottles and bowls are cast in moulds made from the same positives. The bottles originally came as a result of seeing the bottle shape while working on a bowl upside down. The bodies of the pieces have a dry cone 10 reduction-fired glaze made of nepheline syenite, kaolin and silica, textured like fine sandpaper through application by spray gun. The colours are vivid aqua (copper), warm orange rust (iron), bright cobalt blue, and yellow rust (iron). The necks, feet and clipped areas have commercial cone 05 glazes applied to the high-fired pots through heating and spraying. These shiny colours are pink, light blue and pale salmon. The separate areas were masked with liquid latex and/or tape. I view this series of bottles and bowls as geometric constructions and use colour and texture to emphasize this and to make the notion playful.' By STEPHANIE DE LANGE (USA), 1983–5.

Raku bowls with alkaline glaze over white slip inside. The bowl on the left has terra sigillata outside and is a reddish brown in colour, while the one on the right is a bluish, metallic black from a thin wash of copper oxide mixed with glaze. These pieces have been reduced in sawdust immediately on being taken from the kiln. Height of larger bowl 18 cm (7 in). By DIETER BALZER (West Germany), 1986. (Photo: Udo Hesse)

Torn as opposed to cut rims have a more 'natural', organic feeling about them, especially when the clay is reapplied in a different position while it is still wet. This requires a freer, less self-conscious approach from the potter. The 'edge-scape' vessels of **Sally Bowen Prange** (USA) are in direct contrast to the slip-cast bowls of Stephanie De Lange. They appear to have grown into shape rather than to have been manufactured, and her choice of glaze surface emphasizes their organic nature.

'Edge-scape Vessel'. Porcelain bowl with assembled and altered edge under a cratered glaze containing silicon carbide. This piece was inspired by the image of barnacle-encrusted pots salvaged from the sea. Diameter 33 cm (13 in). By SALLY BOWEN PRANGE (USA), 1986. (Photo: Richard Faughn)

Partially thrown bowls which have coils freely added to raise their walls have been explored by a number of potters trying to break away from what they believe to be the formal constraints of the potter's wheel. Two English potters, **Mary White** (now working in West Germany) and **Robin Welch**, both developed their own very distinctive wheel-thrown bowl shapes that became familiar to many during the 1970s and early 1980s. For several years **Robin Welch**, working mainly in a grogged stoneware, produced some powerful bowls which were elevated on a cylindrical foot, with torn rims, and circled by prominent, sharply defined flanges and incised bands. He developed many excellent variations on this theme in his own, unmistakable style. Now, however, he prefers looser forms with irregular surfaces achieved by hand building upon a thrown base. The motivation for this change came from a period Welch spent in the lush tropical landscape of Queensland, Australia. He was deeply impressed by the variety of flora in that part of the country and began to move towards a more organic interpretation of vessel forms.

Links with Welch's previous work do undoubtedly remain and certain design elements, notably the use of horizontal bands of colour and/or texture, continue to accentuate the forms. Many of his new pots are rather like paintings formed into cylindrical, conical or other open shapes of roughly circular section. Partly thrown and partly coiled, these open bowl-like vessels have lost none of the vigour which was such an important feature of his earlier work. There is, also, considerable variety to be seen in the juxtaposition of the colours and textures he uses in an abstract expressionistic manner to complement the form.

A similar, fairly abrupt change of direction in the exploration of bowl forms has been taken by **Mary White**. Wide-flaring, almost flat bowls with a central well and relatively small foot occupied her for several years, but much of her recent work, although still in porcelain, now combines hand building with thin clay sheets, torn rather like paper, onto a thrown base. Tension is maintained, despite the pierced and eroded upper section of the bowl, by following through the upward-curving profile from foot to rim.

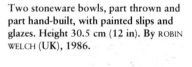

Two stoneware bowls, part thrown and part hand-built, with painted slips and glazes. Height 30.5 cm (12 in). By ROBIN WELCH (UK), 1986.

Above: Group of stoneware bowls on exhibition at the City Museum, Stoke-on-Trent, in 1986. By ROBIN WELCH (UK).
(Photo: City Museum, Stoke-on-Trent)

Large stoneware bowl, thrown and hand-built. Glazed with dolomite and feldspar. Diameter 24 cm (9½ in), height 19 cm (7½ in). By MARY WHITE (UK), 1985.

Some remarkable images have been produced by **Ian Godfrey** (UK), which include animal shapes applied to the rims of vessels, thus creating an unusual horizon line. It is more common to cut surplus clay away from narrow wall sections, to reveal silhouetted elements or deeply undulating rims, because this avoids problems which can arise when joining thin edges together.

The illustrations of bowl forms by **Jenny Welch** (UK) and **Susan Annandale** (South Africa) show two approaches to the rim design. The porcelain piece by **Jenny Welch** is like a delicate, translucent shell offered up on a tall pedestal. The edge is carved into an uneven organic form in sympathy with the chosen material. In comparison, **Susan Annandale**'s bowl has been made in stoneware, which requires a bolder treatment. Her bowl was initially thrown and when it had stiffened sufficiently to hold its shape the rim was softened so that flattened coils of clay could be added and pinched to reach the desired height. The lower part of the bowl was kept damp by wrapping it in polythene sheeting to allow the whole piece to harden and shrink evenly. The rim was eventually cut into shape with a pair of scissors and the wall scraped smooth with a metal tool. The pattern echoing the curvature of the rim was produced with a satin-matt, soda feldspar glaze applied over latex resist on the bisque. The clay body, which is high in iron and manganese, bled through as dark flecks during firing in oxidation to 1300°C.

Stoneware bowl with cut and modelled rim. Diameter 15 cm (6 in) excluding handle. By IAN GODFREY (UK).

Sculptural bowl in porcelain, with fine and fragile edges. By JENNY WELCH (UK).

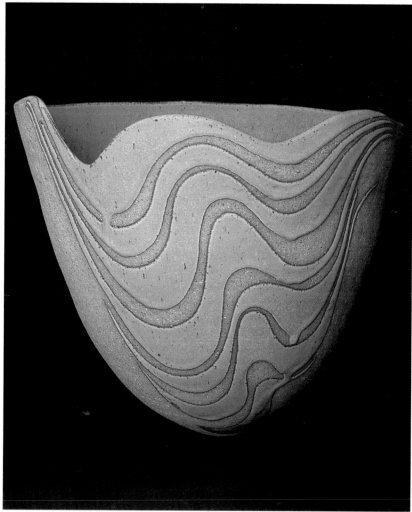

Stoneware bowl with a soda feldspar glaze over a latex resist pattern of undulating lines which echo the cut rim shape. The glaze burns away at the edges leaving a strong brown outline. The body, which is high in iron and manganese, fires to a rich creamy colour at cone 10 and produces the dark flecks in the glaze. Height 48.5 cm (19⅛ in). By SUSAN ANNANDALE (South Africa). (Photo: David Annandale)

The rims of bowls by **Fritz Rossmann** (West Germany) are given emphasis not by carving, but with crisp finishing and by colour or tonal contrast with the main body. This change of colour marks an equally positive change of direction in the profile so that the rim becomes a strong culminating statement to the form. In the pots by **Kevin Boyd** (Australia) rims are flared out horizontally to provide platforms for linear, slip-trailed decoration. These flatter rims have been cut into hexagonal shapes whereas the thickened, hard-edged rim of the thrown bowl by **Vic Greenaway** (Australia) has been altered to form a square opening.

Torn edges are often a feature of the distinctive vessel forms made by **Colin Pearson** (UK) in a vigorous and expressive manner. He has, for many years, explored form through a wide variety of open vessels to which are attached, at opposing sides, two lugs rather like wings or fins. These pieces are thrown then altered, sometimes becoming oval or rectangular in plan, prior to the additions being made. Even when the circular section is retained the added elements transform the vessel into an object which has one major elevation to be viewed with the 'wings' outstretched equally on either side of the body. (Similar shapes with large, modelled, vertical handles on opposite sides were made in China from the Sung period, 960–1279, onwards and are known as *kuei* forms.) Thematic explorations such as this can be both challenging and self-sustaining.

One potter who developed an impressive range of variations within a limited number of specific vessel themes was **Hans Coper** (UK). He considerably influenced the work of many potters in Britain through his pots and by his teaching, but he is rather less well known outside Europe. He was one of those rare individuals whose work will not only withstand the searching test of time but which will continue to affect, indefinitely, the way that many of us approach and respond to pots. With such a vast wealth of ceramic tradition behind us, it is hardly surprising that there are comparatively few contemporary potters who have truly broken fresh ground with such dramatic effect as did Hans Coper. He produced work of great power and originality over a relatively short period before his early death at the age of sixty-one. In many respects his composite forms were new to ceramics even though they were clearly constructed from two or more recognizable geometric shapes. In fact, they are basically simple combinations of cylinders, spheres and circular, triangular or rectangular elements in various juxtapositions. Working in this way might appear to be somewhat mechanical – merely a matter of joining one form to another; but Coper worked with a sharply focused aesthetic awareness and a good helping of intuitive logic.

His pots evolved from the thematic exploration of wheel-thrown forms, but they were by no means limited by the circular section so obtained. For example, cylinders were often reshaped by being squeezed, while still plastic, at the rim to make an oval aperture, or closed completely to form a sharp-edged shoulder. Wide-bellied pots were sometimes altered in similar fashion to create a different form possessing greater surface tension, as if the air contained is held under constant compression. Occasionally, the cylinder would be flattened slightly and joined at the base into a kind of envelope which was then elevated on a cylindrical column. This device of raising the main body of the piece on a plinth, a column, a tall foot or a tapering base is common to much of Coper's work, with many subtle variations within any one family of forms.

His later work is assured and positive, with crisply defined profiles in which form and surface become integrated into a visual and tactile whole. Colour, at first glance, may appear to be minimal, but the surface treatment of many pieces has developed luminous whites, pinks, oranges, rust-reds, browns and greys. Rims are often accentuated with dense manganese black. Alternate layers of oxides and slips, brushed on or into roughened areas, create rich textural qualities in total harmony with the form.

Within any of a dozen or so major themes explored by Coper we can enjoy the changing relationships between the component parts: height to width, foot to rim, the positioning of ribs and flanges, curved and straight lines, convex and concave surfaces, rough and smooth, light and dark. All these are familiar elements of visual expression, yet they are arranged with a conviction and evidence of feeling that gives Hans Coper a deservedly unique position in contemporary ceramics.

Multiple wheel-thrown forms can be joined together in other ways to create a unified, single vessel and **Beate Kuhn** (West Germany) is among the most innovative of modern potters specializing in composite pieces. She makes no attempt to disguise the separate parts employed in the construction, but uses the ridges, where they join and are stacked or overlapped, to accentuate the form rhythmically. Some of her pieces are built up by repeating similar individual units and joining them edge to edge, preserving their identity while producing a totally new form which, although sculptural in concept, also offers functional possibilities.

For **John Ward** (UK) the bowl is a powerful form no matter how simple. Its openness allows him to explore the relationship between inside, outside and rim, while it encloses and cups a volume of space. The hollowness of vessel forms excites him. All his bowls are hand-built and begin with a pinched base. The wall is built up with coils of clay which have been flattened and curved to suit the intended shape. These are left to stiffen on a plaster bat before they are joined to the pot by overlapping the base of any strip applied previously. When complete and leather-hard, his bowls are carefully scraped smooth with a kidney-shaped steel palette and then burnished with a rounded pebble. Sometimes, the wall is cut and rejoined at this stage to form grooves or ridges before the clay dries. Natural forms often display similar patterns of curving lines that he is able to use as a starting point for design. He works on several bowls at any particular time so that he can leave some to stiffen up while he is building others.

This pot combines two simple thrown elements into a strong visual statement. The rim has been distorted to a figure of eight by vertical indentations and those features are accentuated further by dark manganese pigments leading the eye downwards and into the cleft. Large and small versions of this kind of form were made by HANS COPER (UK) from about 1966.
(Photo: Jane Coper)

Hand-built stoneware bowl with green under matt white glaze fired in an electric kiln to Orton cone 8. Note how the bands echo the curvature of the rim and draw attention to the form. Diameter 20 cm (8 in). By JOHN WARD (UK).

Opposite: Stoneware bowl constructed from individually thrown units in a red body fired to 1240°C in an electric kiln. The form is accentuated by horizontal ridges running around the convoluted wall. Height 22 cm (8⅝ in). By BEATE KUHN (West Germany), 1984. (Photo: Jochen Schade)

Occasionally, the actual process of making may cause him to alter or adjust his original concept of the form.

The character of the most simple vessel forms can be drastically altered by adding further elements to them. For example, a broad shoulder or ledge at the top of a bowl is useful for the attachment of overhead handles, which may be made in clay or any other material. Such additions can extend a bowl's occupancy of space quite dramatically and the space between the underside of the handle and the rim becomes an important part of the whole, increasing its sculptural possibilities. The bowl by **Tom Coleman** (USA) (he refers to it as a 'basket') rises conventionally from a low foot-ring to curve precipitously over and inwards at the top with just a thin, raised band to interrupt the profile at the shoulder. Two uncompromising slab lugs project vertically from the rounded crest to receive a bamboo root handle which, although in marked contrast to the taut, full-blown form beneath, is echoed by the runny, tree-like appearance of the glaze.

A more extravagant handle, constructed from sticks and cane, has been attached to unusual, decorative lugs on the bowl (or 'basket') by **Tim Mather** (USA). It seems to bridge the form like a viaduct spanning a gorge. Spaces between the canes, which change in shape and proportion when the piece is viewed from different angles, support this analogy. Mather is interested in 'controlling access to the interior of the bowl, hence the partly covered areas'. The handles are designed to provide a visual bridge linking one side of the bowl with the other, rather than as a means of picking it up.

Porcelain 'basket' with double wall, bamboo root handle, and salt-ash glaze sprayed over coloured slips. Fired in reduction to cone 10. Width 33 cm (13 in). By TOM COLEMAN (USA), 1984. (Photo: Rick Paulson)

Porcelain 'basket', wheel-thrown, with a cut and faceted foot-ring and modelled additions at the rim. The sticks and cane handle makes a powerful statement in bridging the hollow and linking the unusual lugs on opposing sides of the rim. 41×66×30.5 cm (16×26×12 in). By TIM MATHER (USA), 1983. (Photo: Berry Perlus)

Below: Stoneware basket, thrown and modelled, fired to cone 11 in a reduction atmosphere. This piece has been given rich colour and textural interest by sand-blasting the glaze after the final firing. 63.5×51×41 cm (25×20×16 in). By TIM MATHER (USA), 1985. (Photo: Richard Burkett)

The same may be said of the double-walled bowl construction by **Cindy Butler-Jones** (USA), but she has chosen to use flat clay sheet cut to look like metal. In profile it resembles the helmet of an ancient Greek warrior. **Patrick Horsley** (USA), on the other hand, expresses the plastic property of clay in handles which are made from entwined, extruded coils. These handles are mounted as if they were sprung steel stretching and distorting the rim into an oval plan.

Simple additions to or subtractions from a wheel-thrown pot are unlikely to disguise its underlying geometry (and thus its predictability) unless considerable distortion has taken place. Asymmetric pottery vessels, however, are often aesthetically more challenging to make and to view, in the sense that their plan and elevation are not constant. This can be disturbing or exciting.

Most people will admit to feeling slightly uncomfortable and uncertain when they find themselves in strange surroundings, but constant exposure to new ideas encourages the development of flexible attitudes. Such feelings are heightened in the presence of radically different expressions in forms that challenge long-cherished assumptions. In ceramics, certainly, strong passions are aroused and polarized attitudes fiercely defended whenever traditional concepts are threatened. Unfamiliar vessel forms often demand a conscious adjustment in expectation because our images of ceramic vessels are inextricably bound up with domestic function and that usually implies economy of means in answer to need: a direct, simple form where extravagant expression is confined mainly to the surface decoration. Open-mindedness is an admirable attribute but one which is difficult to maintain in the face of any aggressive challenge to convention. European tastes remain, generally, more conservative than those in the United States, where the vigorous work of potters like **Peter Voulkos, Rudy Autio, Kenneth Price, Ron Nagle** and **Jerry Rothman** broke away from European concepts into new ground.

Below right: **Stoneware basket, thrown and altered to an oval section, with a matt wood-ash glaze. Height 41 cm (16 in). By** PATRICK HORSLEY **(USA), 1986.**

Below: **Bowl form with arch. This vessel is double-walled, made by a combination of throwing and hand-building methods in a red, earthenware clay. It has been raku-fired in a propane gas kiln. 33×30.5 cm (13×12 in). By** CINDY BUTLER-JONES **(USA), 1985. (Photo: Dan Gabriel)**

Thrown bowl form with applied pieces
under a glossy monochrome glaze. Diameter
41 cm (16 in). By JERRY ROTHMAN (USA).

Jerry Rothman (USA) has directed his energies towards an exploration
of vessels over the past decade. His thrown bowls, surrounded and supported by modelled chunks of clay, are an adventure into three-
dimensional form emphasized through the use of monochrome glazes. The
nature of his materials affects everything that he does but dictates nothing.
'There is no real, inherent quality in material, only a manufactured convention. If there are any dictates these would be the artistic conception and
the ability to make it happen.' Decoration or surface treatment is always
thoroughly integrated in his work and never applied as if it were a separate
exercise. 'If it is merely decoration it cannot work. Whatever is physically
on the surface must be, and be seen to be, an intrinsic part of the whole.'

For **Roberta Kaserman** (USA) bowls become 'a forum for investigating spatial relationships and ideas related to containment as well as providing a shaped "canvas" to draw and paint upon'. Eggs, domes, labyrinths, architecture, and old tools supply basic ideas for shapes to be incorporated into her work. She describes many of her bowls as 'rocking pieces'. They have rounded bottoms, rather than foot-rings, so that they 'seek their own natural balance if bumped or jarred, whereas a footed piece might fall over'. Again, separate units combine to make one complete form. In this case, though, the elements are assembled *after* firing. The sections are usually thrown, altered and carved. When dry, they are sanded smooth so that no seams or joints are visible, and some parts are sprayed with a ball-milled, porcelain slip. When fired, parts may be coloured with gouache or acrylic paints and the assemblage may also include other non-ceramic materials because Kaserman feels that 'continuing to work after the firing process is crucial to the ongoing development of ideas and imagery within a given piece'. This work is an exploration of the *notion* of a bowl whose simple exterior protects a delicate and complex interior. The *vessel*, in form and concept, continues to be the focus of the work although the implication of function has been abandoned.

Only in the most liberal sense could the pieces by **Michael Chipperfield** (USA) be considered as 'bowls', yet they share similar concerns in the shaping and containment of space. His primary interest is in the interaction between mass and plane. Basically, as he explains, 'the work revolves around contrasts and contradictions: vitrified plane versus friable mass, light against dark, refined dense translucency versus coarse opacity, line opposed to shape, simplicity versus complexity, art versus artlessness, with the ultimate question of implied utility (vessel) versus non-utility (sculpture)'. There remains a tenuous but identifiable connection with vessel form.

Opposite above: 'Blossom'. Sculptural form with slip-cast porcelain bowl supported on an earthenware base. 35.5×18×15 cm (14×7×6 in). By MICHAEL CHIPPERFIELD (USA), 1985.

Opposite below left: 'Meso-Vessel'. Porcelain vessel form mounted on a multi-fired earthenware pyramid. Height 23 cm (9 in). By MICHAEL CHIPPERFIELD (USA), 1985. (Photo: Ron Forth)

Opposite below right: Fragmented bowl construction, saggar-fired in charcoal to cone 8 and assembled with black waxed thread and phoenix palm fronds. Height 23 cm (9 in). By DEBBIE POINTON (New Zealand), 1986. (Photo: Pat Cumming)

Composite form based on a series of porcelain bowl shapes and including other materials such as glass, silicon wafer, bone, wire, acetate and oil. 33×25×20 cm (13×10×8 in). By ROBERTA KASERMAN (USA), 1983.

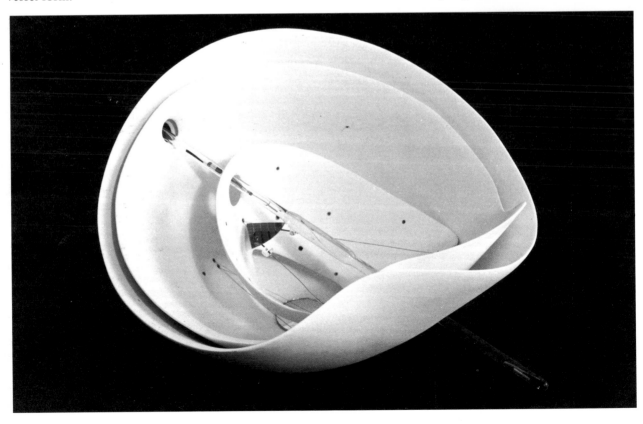

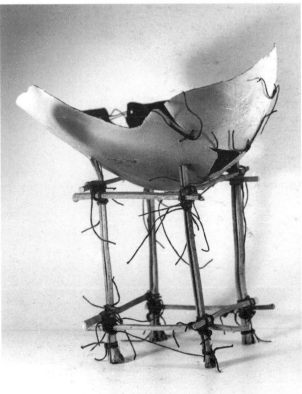

Right: Earthenware vessel form with burnished engobes first fired in a mixture of oxidation and reduction, followed by a second firing in a reducing atmosphere. By PIERRE BAYLE (France).

Far right: Tall vessel form with a pedestal base, 'Alabastre à pied'. Highly polished surface in white earthenware with terracotta engobes. Firing is conducted in an empirical way and the potter judges by the colour of the kiln in the first firing, which is half in oxidation and half in reduction. The second firing is in a reduction atmosphere. Height 41 cm (16 in). By PIERRE BAYLE (France), 1985.

Below: Stoneware bottle vase, hand-built from rolled clay slabs, with matt celadon glaze, fired to cone 11 in reduction in a gas kiln. Height 23 cm (9 in). By WILHELM AND ELLY KUCH (West Germany). (Photo: R. Wiech-Altdorf)

Bottles

The proportions of bottles may be anything between short and fat and tall and slender, and they may be of almost any shape in cross-section. The one common factor uniting vessels within this category is that they are all virtually closed forms, having restricted openings at the top so that very little of the interior can be seen. It might be argued that most bottles should have some kind of neck extending above the main body of the vessel but, for the purposes of this exploration, I am more interested in the body shapes enclosing a volume of space to which there is only limited access. Apart from any decorative value that such forms may possess, bottles can normally be used to store only liquids, granular materials or powders. Yet, for various reasons, ceramic bottles have been largely superseded as functional containers by others manufactured in glass, metals or plastics. Contemporary studio-made glass, especially, has gained in popularity for decorative use, but ceramic bottles still continue to be made and sold in an enormous range of shapes and sizes. In many cases they can be expected to serve no other purpose than to exist as interesting, pleasing and satisfying objects in their own right.

Above: Bottle, thrown and altered, with terra sigillata and incised decoration. Low salt-fired. By GRETE NASH (Norway), 1985. (Photo: Kjartan Bjelland)

Porcelain bottle assembled from three wheel-thrown sections, partly glazed with a white feldspathic glaze under an iron-bearing glaze, fired in reduction to 1360°C. Height 15 cm (6 in). By KARL SCHEID (West Germany), 1979. (Photo: Jochen Schade)

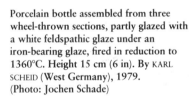

Group of coil-built bottles in red earthenware with metal lustres, smoked in sawdust. By JUDY TRIM (UK), 1983. (Photo: Brian E. Rybolt)

Shaping techniques

Any making method or combination of techniques may be employed in the creation of a bottle, but, since many are wheel-thrown, those of circular section far outnumber any others. In this process the major part of the body must be completed before the neck is collared in and the opening becomes too small to accommodate the potter's hand. Some slight adjustments are still possible after forming the neck, but this requires careful manoeuvring with a rod having a rounded end (or small sponge attached) to stretch the wall outwards as the wheel rotates. A certain amount of reshaping can also be tackled by applying pressure from the outside either with or without internal support. One of my favourite and most versatile tools for this purpose is the flexible, kidney-shaped steel palette which can be bent to match the profile of the pot. Using the same tool just before cutting the pot from the wheel also helps to remove excess moisture or slip from the surface cleanly.

The potter has to bear in mind the amount of clay he will need to retain in the wall for closing in and forming a neck, because collaring the upper part may prove impossible if the wall becomes too thin during throwing. Wider forms, especially, are difficult to collar in at the top without causing diagonal rippling in the wall as the clay particles pile up against each other. To avoid this problem the top may be thrown separately and added later when the main body has stiffened sufficiently to accept the weight. It is also quite common practice to develop the neck section gradually, by adding coils to the top edge. In this way it is possible to continue throwing without the risk of the wall collapsing beneath.

Collaring, at whichever stage, requires both hands to be spread around the circumference of the pot, smoothly squeezing in towards the centre. I

Porcelain bottle, thrown, with smoked terra sigillata surface coloured violet-purple, and orange-brown speckling. Diameter 24 cm (9½ in). **By** JEAN PAUL AZAIS **(France), 1985. (Photo: Paul Palau)**

Stoneware bottles, coil-built, with black feldspathic glaze fired in oxidation to cone 9. Height of tallest piece 45 cm (17¾ in). **By** MAURICE SAVOIE **(Canada), 1965. (Photo: J. P. Beaudin)**

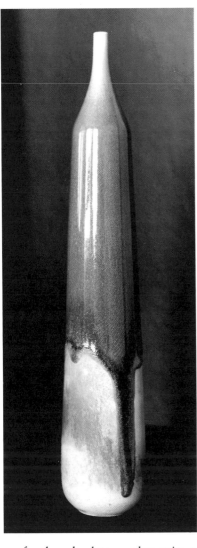

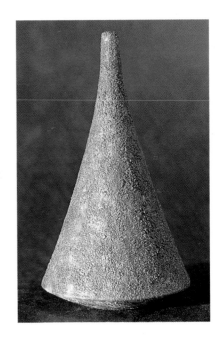

Right: Stoneware bottle, wheel-thrown and first fired to 1240°C in an electric kiln, then low-fired with a borax/copper glaze to 1010°C. By CECILIA PARKINSON (New Zealand), 1986. (Photo: Howard Williams)

Right: Tall bottle of thrown porcelain, having a smoked terra sigillata surface with ivory, green metallic, and brown-violet colours. Height 49 cm (19¼ in). By JEAN PAUL AZAIS (France), 1984. (Photo: Paul Palau)

Left: Tall porcelain bottle, thrown and turned, with a feldspathic glaze applied in varying thicknesses and fired in an electric kiln to cone 7. This is an elegant form, gradually tapering towards the shoulder where the profile changes direction. The flowing glaze accentuates the verticality of the piece. Height 36 cm (14¼ in). By JOCHEN KUHNHENNE (West Germany), 1986. (Photo: Wolfgang Waldow)

prefer the wheel to revolve quite quickly during this movement. Collaring is followed by rethrowing the top section and then the two movements alternate in this way until the desired result is achieved. The wall is thickened during collaring, but throwing makes use of that extra clay to lengthen the wall or extend it upwards into a neck, thinning it at the same time. Water tends to run down the inside of the wall and accumulate at the bottom of the bottle and this must be removed before the neck is completed or the piece will dry unevenly, with a risk of cracks appearing in the base. A sponge on the end of a stick is useful for this purpose when the aperture is too small to allow access to a hand.

Should a bottle form lose its clear profile in the throwing or in the development of a neck, the problem can be solved by blowing into it, like a balloon: the pressure of air from within will often restore the tension and bring the pot to life. (A piece of paper, with a small hole in the middle to blow through, can be placed over the opening by fastidious potters averse to the taste of wet clay!) Another method is to close the form completely so that the volume of air trapped inside serves as a resilient cushion, enabling further adjustments to be safely made to the form from the outside. When stiffened enough to retain its shape, the bottle can be opened up and finished off with or without a neck. The latter can be made separately or added as coils to be shaped directly on the pot.

Stoneware bottle with angular profile, fired in oxidation to cone 10. Height 32 cm (12½ in). By VOLKER ELLWANGER (West Germany), 1968.
(Photo: Hans-Joerg Soldan)

Design influences

The analogy can be easily made between bottle forms and the human figure. There are the obvious references to lips, necks, shoulders, bellies and feet, of course, but the completion of a form with most of these features in approximately similar proportions intensifies the allusion. The pot growing under the potter's hands on the wheel assumes a natural symmetry, but the character projected by a symmetrical bottle is dependent upon the differing proportions of those features and on how they relate together within the whole. Small irregularities can noticeably interrupt the profile of a pot without affecting our understanding of its essentially even balance. On the other hand, positive asymmetry in bottle forms often requires an adjustment of our expectations to a greater extent than in a more open vessel like a bowl, and profiles become less predictable.

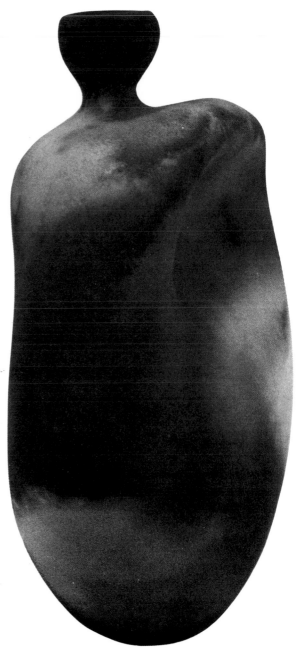

Asymmetric bottle form with smoked surface. By FLOY SHAFFER (USA).

Far left: Stoneware bottle, wheel-thrown and burnished, fired to 1240°C, then placed in a saggar with sawdust, copper oxide, copper sulphate, potassium bichromate and stannous chloride, and fired in a gas kiln to 1000°C to produce a multi-coloured patina. By CECILIA PARKINSON (New Zealand), 1986. (Photo: Howard Williams)

Left: Porcelain bottle, hand-built by folding and joining rolled sheets of clay, with celadon glaze. By VIRGINIA CARTWRIGHT (USA), 1982.

Below: 'Resurgence'. Tall stoneware bottle, wheel-thrown, with painted figure decoration. Height 91 cm (36 in). By ROBERT WASHINGTON (UK), 1985.

Left: Slab-built bottle, constructed from thin sheets of stoneware clay, with sprayed 'carbon trap' glazes over stencil. Height 33 cm (13 in). By PAUL MIKLOWSKI (USA), 1984.

The refined classical shapes of early Oriental vessels continue to provide the bench mark for the vast majority of potters working on the wheel today. While those influences may be easily recognized in an individual's pots, the best work produced by modern potters usually has sufficient input of personal feeling to claim its own identity, even when similar shapes, glazes and colours are used. More especially, the writings of **Bernard Leach**, bridging the cultures of East and West, have had enormous impact on the thinking and attitudes of generations of potters. Certainly, the bulk of functional wares by studio potters in Britain and elsewhere owes much to that particular mix of Oriental and English medieval pottery propagated by the 'Leach tradition'.

Bernard's son, **David Leach** (UK), continues to produce his own distinctive pots within that familiar framework. He feels that a bottle is 'a satisfying form in its own right that can stand alone with some dignity and without any need to relate to function'. His only reservation concerns applied decoration, which he believes should come through the sympathetic use of materials handled with fluent skills. 'Surface brush decoration needs constant practice or fluency is rarely achieved. Without this it tends to be much more "applied", less integrated. I like decoration that reveals evidence of the process which led to its being. Confident and free, not too meticulous and careful.'

Other throwers have found their inspiration elsewhere and most especially from the Middle Eastern and Mediterranean cultures. One potter whose work has been significantly affected through almost two decades of research in the Middle East is **Alan Peascod** (Australia). He feels that it is the attitudes of Middle Eastern potters that have influenced him most of all. Apart from this reference, however, his approach is barely affected by external stimuli because his own ideas, processes and techniques are largely self-sustaining. He deliberately works outside most accepted parameters of ceramic convention and pays scant regard to contemporary fashion as he believes that he has more to learn from working to his own personal vision.

It is difficult for Peascod to ignore the humanoid characteristics of certain container vessels, but, for him, bottle or jar forms are by far the most expressive. 'Style and proportion can become sculptural in orientation when one considers the interplay between positive and negative space such as those areas around the neck, body, handle or spout.' In his own work he regards body and neck as 'secondary components which are only brought into sharp focus by the use of character-forming devices such as the rim, spout, handle, or some other appendage'. It is the endless permutation of these relationships that he finds irresistible. Avoiding the constraints of function allows Peascod to devote all his energies to aesthetic considerations. He uses conventions as a base from which he can systematically push an idea to the very extreme. He has explored ideas where the handle is in fact non-existent, indicated only by vestigial stubs at the points where it might once have been joined to the form. This helps him to create a feeling of greater tension in a piece 'by avoiding a too literal explanation and involving the viewer in the question of what the rest of the handle shape might have been'.

Alan Peascod's adventurous and questioning approach to the processes involved in the creation of ceramics illustrates that traditional techniques may be successfully challenged and even discarded in the search for individual expression. He regularly force-dries his pots with the flame of a gas jet as he works. Stiffening the clay so quickly in this way enables him to engineer extreme angles and structures. It also provides him with the

Two stoneware bottles, both tenmoku-glazed and fired to 1300°C in a reduction kiln. The larger bottle has ilmenite decoration; the smaller one has two thicknesses of tenmoku and wax-resist decoration. Heights 46 cm (18 in) and 30.5 cm (12 in). By DAVID LEACH (UK). (Photo: J. M. Anderson)

Porcelain bottle, wheel-thrown, with incised decoration under a 'manganese gold' brushed slip glaze containing one part copper oxide, seven parts manganese dioxide, and three parts red earthenware clay. Fired to 1260°C in an electric kiln. By PETER BEARD (UK), 1985. (Photo: John Wylie)

'Kashani Metamorphosis IV'. Thrown stoneware bottle form with sgraffito decoration through multiple slips. Height 65 cm (25½ in). By ALAN PEASCOD (**Australia**), 1986.

'Ritual Vessel'. Wheel-thrown piece in sections, with sgraffito and multiple slips under a matt zinc glaze fired to 1250°C (cone 8). Height 52 cm (20½ in). By ALAN PEASCOD (**Australia**), 1986.

facility to 'freeze' a handle or a neck in a position that, under normal conditions, would not be structurally possible. Many of the bottle forms he makes, which are tackled with great vigour and imagination, display a refreshing vitality. Some of the more unusual methods used by Peascod to work on and into the surfaces of his pots are described in Chapter 4.

Variations in simple forms

Bottles swelling out from a small base and restricted by a narrow neck have been popular and useful objects for thousands of years. Among modern potters who have continued to explore the nuances of profile and proportional relationships is **Catharine Hiersoux** (USA) of California. Her pots are taut, full-blown forms with clean, hard lines almost as if they had been turned on a lathe. They present an image of classical simplicity and strength. In the bottles illustrated here there is a relatively sudden change of direction where the inward curve of the shoulder meets the neck and this contributes to the impression that the volume of air within the body is held under intense compression. The eye is prepared for this change with banded accents in the form of one or more turned ridges at this point. The neck then narrows a little further as it soars up and outwards in a natural curve ending at a sharply defined lip.

A similar shape of neck can be seen in the bottle by **Hein Severijns** (Holland), although the main body of his pot is taller in relation to its width. Nevertheless, the profile has a simple and continuous natural curve with a slight suggestion of visual heaviness at the base, where it is wider than at the shoulder. This piece differs further from that of Catharine

Above: Porcelain bottle with aventurine glaze, cream speckle on tan ground, kaki band and glaze spots. Fired in reduction to cone 10 (1300°C). Height 14.5 cm (5¾ in). By DEREK CLARKSON (UK), 1985.

Opposite above: Two thrown porcelain bottles with sharply defined profiles, one with a bright copper-red glaze fired in reduction. Heights 32 cm (12½ in) and 27 cm (10½ in). By CATHARINE HIERSOUX (USA), 1986. (Photo: Richard Sargent)

Opposite below: Porcelain bottle with matt, crystalline glaze fired in oxidation to cone 8. By HEIN SEVERIJNS (Holland), 1985.

Right: Stoneware vessel with painted, metallic lustre decoration. The neck is glazed with a different colour and smooth texture which stops abruptly, but naturally, at the ridge marking the junction at the shoulder. Height 40 cm (15¾ in). By NURIA PIE BARRUFET (Spain), 1986.

Below: Stoneware vessel with a rich visual texture from a combination of tenmoku and ash glazes reduction-fired in a gas kiln to cone 10. By WALTER AND GISELA BAUMFALK (West Germany), 1986.

Hiersoux in that it is elevated on a small foot-ring. Such a device helps to make it appear rather more static.

Thrown bottles, which have a fullness of form rising and expanding from a small base before returning again to an even smaller conclusion, hold a special fascination for **Derek Clarkson** (UK) also. 'A small bottle with a smooth surface and waxy glaze acts as a touchstone. A larger one is also evocative with both masculine and feminine characteristics, and its inner, unseen and almost totally enclosed volume can add a subtle extra dimension.' Although these pieces are undoubtedly bottles, the provision of such narrow openings, as favoured by Clarkson, precludes most of them from having any 'useful' purpose other than their occupation of space.

The bottle by the Spanish potter **Nuria Pie Barrufet** provides us with another variation of that gradual, uninterrupted, curving profile. Again, we see the tiny ridge encircling and emphasizing the junction of shoulder and neck, still curving upwards but only for a short distance. This is accentuated further, but without destroying the unity of the form, by a change in colour.

Stoneware bottle, wheel-thrown, with relief modelling forming two ribs, and dry, black, barium glaze fired in reduction to cone 9. Height 21 cm (8¼ in). By GARRY BISH (Australia), 1985. (Photo: R. Aulsebrook)

Right: 'Sash Bottles'. Marbled stoneware clay bottles, wheel-thrown and fired to cone 9 in reduction. Height 21 cm (8¼ in). By GARRY BISH (**Australia**), 1985. (Photo: Dennis O'Hoy)

Purity of profile is more difficult to achieve when the form is based on a sphere. The slightest deviation of the surface is more noticeable where it interrupts the contour. **Garry Bish** (Australia) has produced some well-defined spherical bottles which, viewed from certain angles, seem to have much in common with the four pieces discussed above. The junction of body and neck in the bottle illustrated (top) is marked in a similar way. The curve of the neck also shares the same basic characteristics, but here the top edge is flattened into an almost completely closed disc. A more unusual feature, however, is the double ridge which runs upwards from near the bottom of the sphere and slopes slightly away from the vertical until it breaches the neck ring. This gives the piece an appearance of having been slashed and the outer skin peeled back. The matt black surface of this bottle has a dry, barium glaze which, being non-reflective, allows the form to be easily understood at a glance.

Bish was first attracted to bottle shapes during the early 1970s when investigating the gold diggings around Bendigo, Victoria. There, he discovered an enormous diversity in size, proportion, shape, colour and decoration among the old, discarded bottles that littered the site. Some were made of glass, others of ceramic, and these finds prompted him to start a collection. His own early work, stimulated by this experience, owed much to the bottles he had found although it was also conditioned by functional requirements. Eventually, he developed many personal variations on a theme of thrown bottles having full, rounded profiles and small necks flattened at the top. He admits that what he finds so appealing in bottle forms is their 'response to exaggeration. There is no form more pleasing to me than one that springs from a small foot, curves into a full belly, and constricts suddenly to a narrow neck.'

Stoneware bottles. By GÖRGE HOHLT (West Germany). (Photo: Rolf Zwillsperger)

Group of three wheel-thrown bottles, decorated with slip-soaked textile fabric and rubbed glaze, with airbrushed ceramic stains. Fired in reduction to cone 9. Height of tallest piece 35.5 cm (14 in). By GARRY BISH (Australia), 1985. (Photo: D. Gibson)

Many potters, whose pots could not possibly be used as containers in the accepted sense, happily produce forms which, nevertheless, possess some of those familiar characteristics we normally associate with the long traditions of ceramic vessels. They might concern themselves with the tensions created by enclosing volumes of space and with the sculptural or painterly approach to the treatment of form and surface. This can result, for example, in wheel-made pots that began as vessels but which were completely closed towards the end of the forming process.

David Kuraoka (USA) of San Francisco is one potter whose forms have a great deal to do with the enclosure and containment of space. The strong, generous curves of his globular pieces seem to suggest that the volume of contained air within is held under great compression. He feels that there is a sense of 'completeness' in these full, rounded forms. Making vessels during his student days was, he believes, a kind of reaction to his avant-garde peer group, which frowned upon traditional pottery as being too restrictive. Since that time his work has evolved into a more personal exploration of form, not limited by the rules of 'useful' pottery. The pieces he makes now are entirely non-functional, yet they retain close ties with traditional forms.

Working almost exclusively with a heavily grogged clay, Kuraoka uses rubber ribs to shape and compress the body. Through a process of burnishing the pot in combination with an engobe, he obtains a smooth, white surface which is ideally suited to pit firing. This method of firing can make somewhat unpredictable marks, colours and visual textures on the pot, but at the same time it allows him to obtain rich and varied surfaces according to his choice of wood, the additions of simple chemical combinations (for example, salt, soda ash, copper oxides), and the length of the firing. Robust, uncomplicated forms are most receptive and suited to this type of firing.

Another potter who is similarly attracted to the full, rounded form and pit-firing techniques is **Ray Rogers** of New Zealand. Like David Kuraoka, he chooses the word 'completeness' to describe his feeling for these shapes. Almost all his pots are wheel-thrown and then worked on later when they have stiffened. The surfaces are smooth and uninterrupted in the curve from base to neck. Sometimes, textured detail, suggested by the patterns of coral or fungi, encircles a small opening at the top. A final accent such as this gives the pot added interest and helps to emphasize the tautness of its surface and the feeling of compression within. Again, the burnished outer skin of the piece presents a clear and expansive area to the free-moving action of the flames.

The pit or trench used by Ray Rogers is about 4.5 m (5 yd) long, 1.5 m ($1\frac{3}{4}$ yd) wide, and 1.5 m ($1\frac{3}{4}$ yd) deep. The pots (having been bisque-fired previously to a temperature of 750°C in a gas kiln) are placed on a bed of sawdust about 20 cm ($7\frac{3}{4}$ in) deep at the bottom of the trench. Clean, dry wood is then stacked carefully and directly on top of them to a depth of between 0.5 m ($\frac{1}{2}$ yd) and 1 m (1 yd). The pit is covered with sheets of corrugated iron to enclose it and give Rogers some degree of control over the firing, which takes between four and five hours (this usually includes some restoking). The corrugated iron sheets are also used to close up the pit completely when the firing is finished. They are left in place for a period of about twenty-four hours, by which time the pots are cool enough to remove safely.

Small amounts of oxides may be sprayed onto the pots before firing and salt can be scattered among them in the pit to encourage the development of colours. Copper carbonate is volatile and its fumes give reds, pinks and

Above: Large spherical pot, wheel-thrown and pit-fired, with colours obtained from the type of wood used, together with additions of simple chemicals (salt, soda ash, copper), and the length of firing. David Kuraoka grew up on the small, lush island of Kauai, Hawaii, and is greatly influenced by the beauty found in nature. Misty landscapes, rock formations, rough, craggy mountains and tropical beaches all provide sources for his imagery. 51×28 cm (20× 11 in). By DAVID KURAOKA (USA), 1984. (Photo: Dean Oshiro)

Large pit-fired vessel (porous and non-functional) with 'fungoid' decorative treatment in relief. Diameter approximately 38 cm (15 in). By RAY ROGERS (New Zealand), 1984. (Photo: Peter Colville)

Porcelain vessel with lid. 44×34 cm (17¼×13½ in). By JOHN TAKEHARA (USA), 1983.

Below left: Three large coil-built bottles, raku-fired. Maximum width 58 cm (22¾ in) and maximum height 60 cm (23½ in). By DAVID ROBERTS (UK), 1986.

Below: Stoneware bottle, wheel-thrown and altered to an oval section, ash-glazed and fired to 1350°C. The throwing rings add interest to the surface and draw attention to the oval nature of the form. Height 43 cm (17 in). By GÖRGE HOHLT (West Germany), 1982. (Photo: B. Deller-Leppert)

soft pastel colours, while cobalt and chrome oxides produce blues and greens respectively. Iron oxides react with salt to give shades of orange. Intense blacks to delicate greys develop from the carbon absorbed from burning sawdust. Flames, smoke, and the passage of air all contribute to the fairly random swirls of colours and tones that enliven the surface of pots fired in this way.

Spherical pots of an impressively large size are also made by **John Takehara** (USA) from Boise, Idaho. He usually throws these pots in one piece from approximately 25 kg (55 lb) of porcelain clay. This large mass of clay is thrown in a slow and deliberate manner. When the wall of the bottle has been raised sufficiently, curving out and upwards, the top edge is compressed and collared in gradually. It is then allowed to stiffen a little before coils of clay are added, smoothed into each other and thrown again to complete the form with a small opening at the top. If the pot becomes distorted around the shoulder during the final stages of throwing, it is inflated, literally, by blowing air into it, as described earlier, so that it swells up to describe a full, firm contour. These simple, yet powerful shapes are typical of Takehara's work and a similar feeling for taut rotundity can be seen in most of his pieces. Even his taller, lidded jars are often variations of the same concept, except that they are higher in relation to their width and have a slightly raised neck-ring to hold the lid securely.

Thrown pots can be altered from the round section by being beaten with a wooden paddle when almost leather-hard to make a number of flattened faces. This method produces a different kind of angularity from what might be achieved by cutting slices from the thickness of the wall. Another option is to cut away a leaf-shaped piece from the centre of the pot floor, while the clay is still fairly soft, and to push the sides inwards, rejoining the cut edges. This forces the pot into an oval section and broadens its lower wall. Beating the wall when it has stiffened a little helps to refine the form. The top edge is then moved into an interesting curve, especially where the neck culminates in a wide-flaring lip on a bottle altered to an oval section from the round. Some of the best examples of this feature can be seen in bottles by **Lucie Rie** (UK), who throws the necks separately and slightly flattens them below the flared lip.

Another method of faceting the walls is to slice through the 'cheeks' of a full-blown bottle so that, by reversing and rejoining the cut pieces in the same positions, a dramatic and deeply dimpled form can be made.

Porcelain vessel with carved top and sides and semi-matt crystalline glaze. By INGVIL HAVREVOLD (Norway), 1985. (Photo: Teigens Fotoatelier)

Far left: Tall stoneware pot, wheel-thrown and altered. By JOANNA CONSTANTINIDIS (UK). (Photo: Crafts Council)

Left: Stoneware bottle with slightly flattened neck which has caused the lip to distort to an interesting undulation. By LUCIE RIE (UK). (Photo: Crafts Council)

Pillow-shaped bottles can be produced from two 'bee-hive'-shaped pots joined together rim to rim and turned sideways to receive a separately thrown foot and neck. This kind of form provides a broad platform for poured and trailed glazes that will flow and encircle the body.

Slab building methods offer, perhaps, the best opportunities for the exploration of bottle forms that have two or more definite sides to them, and there are many ways such projects can be tackled. For example, matching slabs which have been press-moulded into dished shapes can be joined rim to rim to create the body. This can be supported upon a foot of one kind or another and an opening can be made at the top ready for the addition of a neck. Such vessels then present at least two distinct faces on which to display pattern, texture or colour. Where the joined edges of two dish shapes form a definite ridge or spine, a natural perimeter for applied design is provided. Most of **James Tower**'s (UK) work is executed in this way, using pressed, dished slabs that allow him to approach the surface

Slab-built bottle with square base and layered, rust-red tenmoku glaze fired to cone 10. Height 13 cm (5 in). By HORST KERSTAN (West Germany).

Earthenware vessel, press-moulded in two sections, with sgraffito decoration through dark brown glaze on fired white glaze. Height approximately 51 cm (20 in). By JAMES TOWER (UK), c. 1983.

Below: Slab-built bottle form in porcelain with textural pattern produced by painting oxides on the surface of a clay slab which is then stretched by further rolling. Height 23 cm (9 in). By GORDON COOKE (UK), 1986.

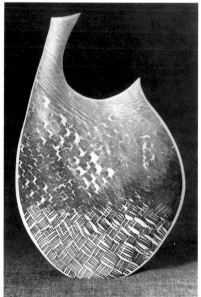

Left: Stoneware bottle form, of slab-built construction, sprayed with a black glaze. This unusual piece is one of many explorations of 'bottle' forms by Paul Miklowski, to whom bottles appeal through an implied reference to the human figure. It is the sculptural aspect and not function that interests him. Height 53 cm (21 in). By PAUL MIKLOWSKI (USA), 1985.

An unusual bottle constructed from slabs of stoneware clay and sprayed with a dense black glaze. Height 48 cm (19 in). By PAUL MIKLOWSKI (USA), 1985.

treatment of each side rather as a painter might tackle a picture. He is able to 'tie' his designs to that continuous, peripheral edge and thus achieve complete integration of form and surface.

More complex variations on the theme of bottles

Flat slabs, which are to be joined together when leather-hard, are used mainly in the production of vessels having rectangular or triangular sections. Thrown or hand-built necks can be added and the permutation of variables is infinite. Stiffened slabs can also be cut into quite complex shapes to be assembled into hard-edged and more unusual bottle forms. **Paul Miklowski's** (USA) stoneware bottles are constructed from flat slabs no more than 7 mm ($\frac{1}{4}$ in) thick and without using any internal supports. He feels that 'no matter how decorative or asymmetrical or sculptural a hollow clay form may be, if it has an opening to the interior it will function as a vessel, although that may be only in some obscure way. But close the form up and, suddenly, our approach to it, and the criteria we rely on to appraise its success as an object that does not even suggest function, have to be modified.' He aims for a total integration of shape and surface in his work through the use of monochrome glazes.

Stoneware vessel form constructed from
wheel-thrown sections. Height 35.5 cm
(14 in). By HANS COPER (UK).
(Photo: Peter Lane)

Composite vessel form, wheel-thrown
stoneware. Height 30.5 cm (12 in). By HANS
COPER (UK). (Photo: Peter Lane)

Philippa Cronin (UK) also chooses flat slabs with which to explore the soaring quality of a vessel or object that stands on a relatively small base and employs the figurative aspects of foot, body and neck. Her work has been heavily influenced by working in metal and she feels that the respective methods of fabrication possess certain similarities. Her own fascination with cubism and illusion is also illustrated by the way in which she uses flat areas of colour to create a sense of ambiguity. Her pots have flat surfaces juxtaposed with curved and twisting edges, and sometimes they are beaten into more extreme shapes that would be difficult to achieve by slabbing alone. Recently, her work has moved away from the traditional concept of a bottle so that she now concentrates more upon exploring the interaction of planes and forms.

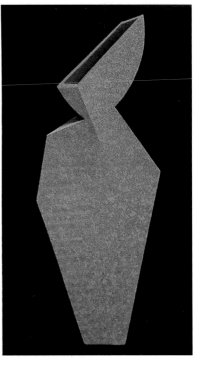

Above: Vessel in grogged, red earthenware clay. Slab- and coil-built and beaten to modify curves. Coloured with blue and yellow slips. Height 55 cm (21½ in). By PHILIPPA CRONIN (UK), 1984.

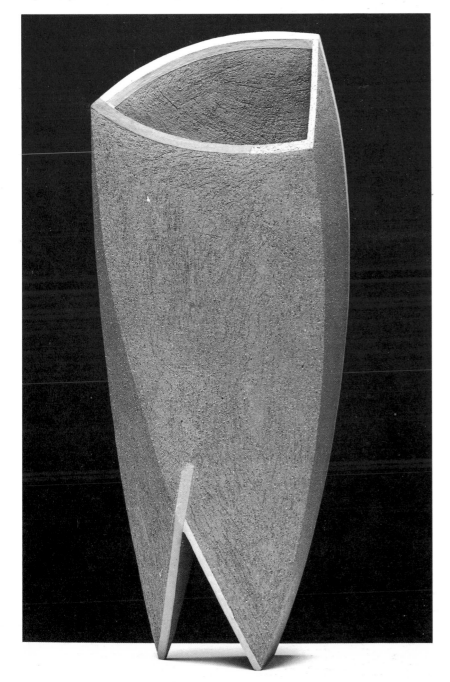

Vessel in grogged red earthenware clay, slab- and coil-built and beaten to modify curves. Coloured with pink and blue-grey slips. Height 48 cm (19 in). By PHILIPPA CRONIN (UK), 1985. (Photo: David Ward)

Opposite above: **Hand-built stoneware bottle, the surface of which is broken into strong angular relief. Height 38 cm (15 in).** By INGEBORG AND BRUNO ASSHOFF (**West Germany**), 1981. (Photo: Bernd Kirtz)

A more gentle use of slabs can be seen in the work of the West German potters **Bruno** and **Ingeborg Asshoff**. Their tall, four-sided earthenware bottle (made in 1966) is a harmonious arrangement of sloping angles. The main body is elevated on an inward-tapering pedestal, and the profile executes a sharp change of direction where that junction occurs. The bottom edge slopes up and away from this point for approximately the same distance as the height of the foot, before another positive directional movement takes place. The main body of this piece, with its broader face inclined inwards from the vertical, soars up to meet a steep shoulder terminated by a tall and narrow cylindrical neck. This beautifully proportioned vessel has a satisfying firmness about it. If I were to express any personal reservation it would concern the neck, which I feel should taper inwards a little more to be in closer sympathy with the rest of the form; but this is a very minor criticism. The later stoneware bottle (made in 1981) demonstrates a more adventurous approach to the bottle form. Terraced planes and angular divisions break up the surface, but the profile at its widest dimension remains basically simple. This later piece presents an image of massive solidity, despite its moderate size, but it is arguable whether the addition of a conventional neck complements the sculptural qualities of the body.

The coil-built vessels by **Rick Rudd** (New Zealand) also exploit the sculptural potential of clay. Sharply defined ledges swirl around and into his forms as if in constant motion. This curving, linear movement is picked out in glaze that contrasts with the coarse texture of the heavily grogged body. The profile of the piece illustrated here is undeniably shaped like a bottle – it is a hollow vessel with a foot, a belly, a shoulder and a neck – but it is, in essence, more of an exploration of the *idea* of the bottle form without regard to any functional application.

Opposite below left: **Earthenware bottle form, with manganese addition to the clay and sgraffito decoration through the glaze. Height 90 cm (35½ in).** By INGEBORG AND BRUNO ASSHOFF (**West Germany**), 1966. (Photo: Dagmar Grauel)

Opposite below right: **Raku vessels in pinched, coiled and scraped white stoneware clay with added grog. Parts of the surface have been smoothed in preparation for the crackle glaze and some areas were burnished and smoked as a contrast to the textured surface. Fired to 1050°C in a gas kiln and then smoked in sawdust. Height of taller vessel 32 cm (12½ in).** By RICK RUDD (**New Zealand**), 1985. (Photo: Ces Thomas)

Right: **Stoneware vessel, wheel-thrown in two sections, with brown engobe under a dry white glaze on the body. The upper section and interior are glazed reddish-brown. Fired to cone 8 in an electric kiln. Height 28 cm (11 in).** By LUCETTE GODARD (**Spain**), 1985. (Photo: Paco Junquera)

Tall bottle vase, coil-built in a coarse stoneware body into which have been wedged manganese and iron oxides; black glazed interior. The surface was scraped when dry to reveal the texture with the lines incised and white engobe brushed over the whole form. The pot was fired to cone 6, the black areas were brushed on, then the pot was refired, also to cone 6. This piece expresses the artist's interest in creating bottle forms 'that swell and constrict in space', and although some sense of function is maintained he is concerned mainly with the development of a sculptural idea. Height approximately 46 cm (18 in). By LARRY ELSNER (USA), 1985.
(Photo: Andrew M. Whitlock)

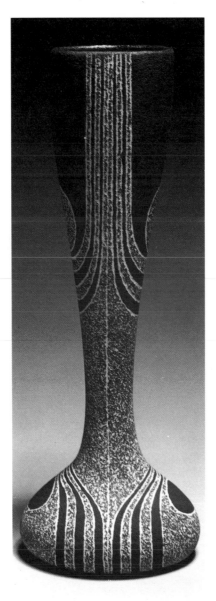

Below: Coil-built stoneware bottle with sgraffito pattern through black engobe. Height 30.5 cm (12 in). By LARRY ELSNER (USA), 1985.

Bottle form, coil-built from coarse clays, with applied engobes and colours obtained from iron and manganese oxides. Fired to cone 6 in oxidation. 24×46 cm (9½×18 in). By LARRY ELSNER (USA), 1985.

Similar concern for form and surface is revealed in the coiled pots by **Larry Elsner** (USA). His pieces are developed primarily as unglazed, sculptural forms, but some sense of function is usually maintained. As a boy, he lived in an area of America where the native stone was of volcanic origin and this has influenced his preference for comparable textures and the use of earth colours in his work. He adds perlite (a white volcanic glass commonly sold in plant and garden stores as an additive to loosen soils for pot plants) to an already coarse clay mixture so that, by scraping the surface when dry, a rich and even texture can be produced. Once the surface has been scraped, linear patterns are scratched onto the pot with a needle. Oxide colours are brushed over and into these marks prior to firing (at cone 6 in an oxidizing atmosphere), perhaps several times before the final colour is resolved. Sometimes, those colours are altered further by hand-grinding areas of the surface after firing. This lightens their value and serves to smooth the body of the pot.

Coarsely grogged clays like this have a satisfying 'tooth' which makes them particularly suitable for building large vessels whose interest depends on form aided by the textural qualities of the clay, rather than on subsequent applications of colour or glaze. Pots intended for use in gardens and conservatories are especially suited to being fashioned in this material and the coil-built pots by **Jenifer Jones** (UK) are evidence of this. Although her pot illustrated here is not, strictly speaking, a bottle form, it does share some common features. It has a relatively small base supporting a full-bellied form which is gathered sharply to a short neck and a flared lip. Two incised lines band the pot where the profile changes direction, while vertical lines are scored down from the neck to stop at the lower band. The groggy nature of the clay is apparent even though the pot was smoothed before the pattern was incised.

Earthenware bottle form, hand-built, with glazes and oxides fired by raku technique. Height 30.5 cm (12 in). By MONIQUE FERRON (Canada), 1976.

Garden pot, coil-built in stoneware clay with bronze and black colour, fired to 1260°C. Height 53 cm (21 in). By JENIFER JONES (UK). (Photo: Lawrence Gresswell)

Large, coil-built, spherical bottle form in low-fired earthenware with burnished surface and a distinctive neck. By MAGDALENE ODUNDO (UK), 1985.

Coil-built, low-fired, earthenware vessel with burnished surface. By MAGDALENE ODUNDO (UK), 1985.

The pots by **Magdalene Odundo** (UK) are very different in concept and execution. She also hand-builds generously rounded, symmetrical shapes to begin with, but she then develops tall, well-defined necks that give them distinctive characters. She uses sharp ridges to describe strong linear movement around the upper form, while concave planes between them provide an interesting, complementary contrast to the spherical body beneath. Her bottle forms, with their direct simplicity and unimpaired surface burnished to a smooth sheen, exert a powerful presence.

The type of clay body, the proportion of grog or sand it contains, and, more especially, the moisture content when the pot is formed all impose restrictions as well as offer opportunities for the potter. The methods used in the construction of a pottery vessel also contribute a great deal to its final character. The wetter the clay, the more likely it is to respond to, and retain evidence of, pressure from within or without during manufacture. Forms are likely to appear looser and more organic than those made with

Above: Bottle constructed from inlaid sheets of coloured clay cut and folded. Fired to cone 5, unglazed. Height 25 cm (10 in). By VIRGINIA CARTWRIGHT (USA), 1986. (Photo: Claire Henze)

Three bottle forms, hand-built by folding and joining rolled sheets of clay. Unglazed and wood-fired. Height of tallest piece 35.5 cm (14 in). By VIRGINIA CARTWRIGHT (USA), 1985.

coils or from stiffened clay sheets. Most of the vessels made by **Virginia Cartwright** (USA), for example, are made from fairly soft slabs of plastic clay. The rolled slabs she uses are cut, overlapped and joined together to create forms in which no attempt is made to disguise the direct and simple building methods involved. The soft, plastic nature of clay remains clearly visible in the hard, fired pot. Here, the process of creation has dictated the character of the pot as much as the relative proportions of the form itself.

Whether functional or merely decorative, and whatever the nature of the materials chosen or the methods used to give physical substance to an individual's concept of form, the final piece must stand as an object in its own right. The work is more likely to succeed if the combination of those materials and processes is appropriate for the idea and has been handled with skill and sensitivity by the potter. But it is the resolution of the form and the communicative power of the image itself that is paramount.

3. DESIGN

Painters and sculptors take their inspiration from any sources that they feel are appropriate, and potters are no exception to this. Much of their basic impetus may well come from exposure to the vast collections of ceramics from all over the world, but although many craftsmen and women do gain an endless stream of ideas through studying pottery from the past or the present, their best works should be far more than a mere pastiche of pieces from history. The objects from their workshops ought to have acquired a separate identity that reflects the time, place and personality of their maker.

Museums and galleries with ceramics collections are readily accessible in most towns and cities and some of these are noted for specializing in a particular aspect of the subject. Anyone who visits the Archaeological Museum in Heraklion, Crete, for example, is likely to be overwhelmed by the vitality, versatility and skill of the Minoan craftsmen as demonstrated mainly by the wonderful collection of magnificent pots. I found it also to be a very humbling experience. We modern potters have so much more technology at our disposal today, yet how rarely can we aspire to such heights as reached by those early artists.

Earthenware bowl with red lustre decoration over tin glaze. Decorated by Passenger at William de Morgan's pottery in the early 20th century.
(Photo: City Museum, Stoke-on-Trent)

Thrown porcelain bowl with a high foot-ring. The crackled glaze is stained yellow by uranium pentoxide fired in oxidation to cone 8. Diameter 23 cm (9 in). By THELMA MARCUSSON (South Africa).

Opposite: 'Ritual Pouring Form'. Wheel-thrown and modelled piece, with 24-carat gold lustre and bronze patina. Height 50 cm (19¾ in). By ALAN PEASCOD (Australia), 1986.

Other potters, too, will freely admit that ancient ceramics often leave them with deep impressions that strongly influence their work. For instance, it was to be a short holiday in Crete and contact with the ancient Minoan culture through its pots, together with visits made to sites at Knossos and Phaestos, that provided **John Chipperfield** (UK) with the inspiration that led to an interesting series of large raku bowls. Elements of design noted during his visit were absorbed to emerge later in a fresh way as features of his own work. The two dominant handles attached to opposing sides of the shallow bowl illustrated here owe much to his appreciation of Minoan vessels. Responding to ceramics of the past like this is an act of re-creation, not imitation.

Opposite: 'Tripod Vessel and Stand'. With blue-green glazes and green terra sigillata. 'My tripod vessels draw aesthetic sustenance from, and try to make meaningful connections to, certain ancient vessel traditions. They are celebrations of containers, with their fundamental characteristics and cultural manifestations. Although my work seeks these archaic roots, I have tried to create a personal, visual vocabulary. The tripod series is an attempt to integrate my sense of sculptural form and space within the pottery context.' Height 55 cm (21½ in). By RICHARD HIRSCH (USA), 1986.

Top: Large, shallow bowl, raku-fired, with applied handles inspired by a study of Minoan pottery. Diameter 46 cm (18 in). By JOHN CHIPPERFIELD (UK), 1986.

Above: Shallow, conical bowl, raku-fired, mounted on four raised, slab feet. Diameter approximately 38 cm (15 in). By JOHN CHIPPERFIELD (UK), 1986.

Shallow stoneware bowl with applied handles. Feldspar and wood-ash glaze with leaf decoration. Diameter 50 cm (19¾ in). By PAUL SPOONER (Australia), 1985. (Photo: Michael Kluvanek)

Hand-made Mimbres bowl, painted earthenware. Diameter 15 cm (6 in). In the collection of William Hunt (USA).

The editor of the American magazine *Ceramics Monthly*, **William Hunt** (USA), is a potter who has always preferred making and looking at bowls to any other ceramic form. Some years ago, when he was visiting Philadelphia, he came upon a painting gallery that sold a few pre-Columbian and southwest American Indian works upstairs in some dusty back rooms. In a far corner of an old packing case he discovered a small Mimbres bowl of compelling geometric design that had been shattered and reassembled. 'But the power of this piece,' he said, 'spoke right through the reconstruction of its parts. If a piece of clay from eight hundred years ago can speak through the ages at all, then this piece virtually shouted at me. I bought it and it has demanded to be my standard ever since. To look at this bowl one sees an extremely casual approach to pottery making. There's so much process showing that it is easy to see most of how the piece was made and a great deal about how the artist felt about the work. There is a small place where some slip was just wiped off a finger onto the bowl, and there is an extremely casual placement of stairstep designs; one senses something of the crude yucca brush used to decorate this piece, which was probably buried over the face of a dead loved one. If such a bowl was not holy in its original use, it is now, simply through the time that it bridges. There is something inevitably spiritual about feeling the feelings of a potter, long dead, through the mark of his/her hand on a bowl floating in our culture: a civilization he/she could barely imagine.'

Hunt believes that one of the best things about making bowls is that because the constraints of function are minimal he is encouraged to experiment widely with all kinds of unusual materials. 'Every material has some optimum use, and the more inventive you are, the more likely you are to find that optimum use. I will accept a great deal of working difficulty in exchange for material beauty in itself.' For example, he has often thrown bowls made from an abrasive mixture of 50 per cent expanded perlite and 50 per cent clay. This body has an extremely coarse texture ('you can't throw many pots without scouring off your fingerprints') and the pitted surface is partly concealed under a glaze that makes the pots appear almost volcanic in origin.

Direct references to earlier works can be identified throughout the long history of ceramics. Inspiration has also been drawn from many different sources and from objects fashioned in other materials. Some ancient pottery vessels can be seen closely to resemble shapes previously produced in metal, and even the decoration of these pots was invariably derived from the same source.

Above: 'The Last Little Human'. Stoneware bowl sculpture set in sand and enclosed in a Plexiglass box. The bowl is constructed with press-moulded clay slabs and the joints and textures are accentuated by rubbing in iron and cobalt oxides. By ULLA VIOTTI (Sweden), 1981. In the collection of the Röölesska Museum, Gothenburg. (Photo: Jöunous Gilder)

Unglazed stoneware bowl with manganese oxide accentuating the textural qualities of the clay. 32×29 cm (12½×11⅜ in). By YVETTE MINTZBERG (Canada), 1985.

Salt-glazed stoneware bowl with perlite additions to the clay. Hand-built, with tripod foot. Diameter 51 cm (20 in). By WILLIAM HUNT (USA), 1984.

Although nature offers limitless images and ideas for design, the search for inspiration need not be confined to a single area such as this because we are usually surrounded by an infinite number of man-made forms in architecture, machinery, vehicles, boats and so on, that can serve in various ways to prompt the imagination. Certain architectural elements which I have seen in ultra-modern buildings in cities like Melbourne, Sydney, Vancouver, San Francisco and Los Angeles have begun to appear in some of my recent work, almost unconsciously, in the form of grid-like, rectilinear patterns. Enormous visual interest can be created by the repetition of a single design unit used in any number of different ways. This is an aspect of both natural and man-made designs that appeals to my own sense of order and has become an integral part of my work.

'City Grid'. Wheel-thrown porcelain bowl with airbrushed ceramic stains in blues and pinks, fired in an electric kiln to cone 8. Diameter 30.5 cm (12 in). By PETER LANE (UK), 1986.

The 'bowls' of water towers at Alençon, France. There are many interesting vessel-like forms to be seen in the wide architectural variety of water towers. (Photo: *The Guardian*)

A student of mine once discovered a rich vein of visual stimulus during a study she was making of those man-made structures which impose themselves on flat landscapes such as those found in East Anglia. Electricity pylons, church towers, windmills and grain silos punctuate the Norfolk countryside around, but she found herself increasingly drawn in particular to the powerful shapes, and considerable variety of design, to be seen in water towers. Her imaginative and thorough research provided a great fund of positive ideas that led directly into work with clay. The pieces she produced were deeply personal and highly original in both concept and execution. Tall vessel forms possessing strong visual and tactile interest echoed, but did not imitate, the source of her inspiration. She had been able to harness her responses to the initial stimulus and to adjust her thinking to suit the requirements of the ceramic medium.

Large stoneware bottle forms designed as candle holders for Lincoln Cathedral. Height of pieces varies between 91 cm (36 in) and 152 cm (60 in). By ROBIN WELCH (UK). (Photo: Chris Goddard)

One method which I enjoy and often use for exploring the concepts of form has also proved helpful to my students. Faced with the problem of visualizing three-dimensional form on paper, one *can* work in line, but I feel that this is often inhibiting and can sometimes be a lengthy process. I prefer to work from and through a series of silhouettes cut from black paper and displayed against a white background. This is particularly suitable when exploring vessel forms because the paper can be folded in half and, by holding the folded edge in one hand, the full profile can be cut from the outer edge in one movement. Symmetry is achieved very easily without the struggle that freehand drawing would demand. More importantly, silhouettes thus created may be interpreted in scores of different ways. The shapes can be explored further by cutting them vertically or horizontally and overlapping the two halves to reduce the size and alter the overall proportions. This will also affect the relationship between the various sections, and other adjustments may therefore be necessary to maintain the aesthetic balance. Another option is to expand the shape in one or other direction by inserting an extra piece of black paper between the cut halves. A related 'family' of forms can be developed quite quickly in this way.

I have used this technique during demonstrations in Britain, America and Australia to stimulate ideas and to challenge conventional ways of thinking and seeing. It has provoked lively discussions and revealed fascinating possibilities for three-dimensional exploration that would not have occurred any other way. The method is discussed in greater detail in Chapter 5, which also features a 'library' of shapes produced by the means described.

In an earlier chapter I mentioned that I believe pots to be like people. We are attracted to some and not to others; just as personal 'tastes' in people will vary from one individual to another so will our responses to pots differ. Bottle forms are more 'complete' and useful in making this analogy. There are, however, certain criteria concerning proportional relationships that are often applied subconsciously in making such judgements. A shorter neck, a higher foot, or a more steeply sloping shoulder on a pot can make us feel either more comfortable or uneasy, according to the altered relationship which is thus made to the rest of the form.

In one interesting experiment I put the same question on separate occasions to three different groups of students at a retrospective exhibition of the work of **Hans Coper** (UK). Three of his vessels were displayed side by side in sole occupancy of a well-lit glass case. All were thematically related in shape, having a thrown body closed at the rim to make a sharp-ridged shoulder with a neck centrally placed on top (see illustrations, right). I asked the students to look carefully at these pots and to choose one which they preferred above the others. Without exception they all chose the same piece: C. In the ensuing discussion the consensus arrived at was that the shoulders of **A** were rather too hunched up, **B** had a disconcertingly long neck, awkwardly related to the body, whereas C had a more 'comfortable' feeling about it. Armed with this unanimous judgement, I put the same question to a group of ordinary people, several of whom were retired. They were volunteer guides to the exhibition and I had just conducted a workshop on Hans Coper for them. All chose C except for one elderly woman who selected **B**. Surprised, and almost without thinking, I blurted out, 'You must have lived in Africa.' 'Yes,' she replied. It seemed that she had often seen giraffe-necked women on her travels and what everyone else had decided were unusual proportions in that particular pot had not disturbed her in the least.

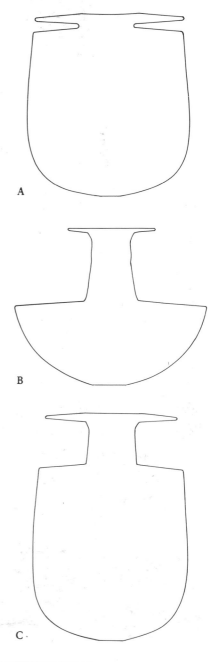

Silhouettes of vessels by Hans Coper.

A

B

C

Ribbed bottle form, wheel-thrown porcelain, with zinc barium glaze containing copper oxide. Fired in oxidation to cone 9 (1280°C). By RAY SILVERMAN (UK), 1985.

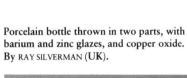

Three stoneware bottles, slab-built, with matt celadon glaze fired in reduction (gas kiln). These pieces illustrate some variations on a simple theme. Height of tallest bottle 43 cm (17 in). By WILHELM AND ELLY KUCH (West Germany). (Photo: R. Wiech-Altdorf)

Porcelain bottle thrown in two parts, with barium and zinc glazes, and copper oxide. By RAY SILVERMAN (UK).

Even though many functional vessel forms evolved into specific shapes long ago, there is still infinite room for individual interpretation in all of them. Potters can explore a whole range of expression merely by continuing to make small adjustments to the profile of a pot spinning under their hands on the wheel, while attempting to retain the volume of its inner space. Similarly, while potters are using hand-building methods, singly or in combination, there will always be opportunities to shift the emphasis and to accentuate or alter the basic character of a pot. Virtually any additions to, or subtractions from it will affect the profile for good or ill. Individual strengths and limitations are soon discovered, so that potters learn not only which shapes give them the greatest pleasure but also how best to express their personal feeling for form.

Some individual approaches to the thematic exploration of bottle forms can be seen in the work of **Wilhelm** and **Elly Kuch** from West Germany. Only very slight differences exist in the basic shapes of the three bottles photographed together here, but the addition of winged lugs at the junction of the shoulder and neck on two of these, in association with the

variations in size and colour, creates extra interest within this related group. A similar development is illustrated in the more loosely fashioned bottle forms by **Dieter Balzer** (West Germany), while the attachment of another kind of decorative lug to the top of the bottle by **Peter Beard** (UK) dictates much of the pot's character. Similar features can form the basis of a visual theme. Limiting the design options to a simple addition or other device often provides the impetus for further developments. Self-imposed constraints of this kind, whether in regard to a specific form or a style of decoration, can certainly lead the way to new ideas. The essential discipline and focus involved help to concentrate the mind so that the exercise can be inspirational and rewarding.

The shapes of many ceramic vessels are often similar, albeit on a different scale, to industrial containers of one sort or another. Parallels can be found also in the details, shapes and forms of other familiar objects, large and small. Exploring areas of design unconnected with pots often opens up fresh veins of stimulating thought from which may emerge ideas for new shapes and patterns.

Above: Porcelain bottle, wheel-thrown, with incised decoration under a 'manganese gold' brushed slip glaze containing one part copper oxide, seven parts manganese dioxide, and three parts red earthenware clay, fired to 1260°C in an electric kiln. Height 20 cm (8 in). By PETER BEARD (UK), 1985. (Photo: John Wylie)

Left: Four raku bottles, hand-built, with black body colour and tops of turquoise or silver from alkaline glaze containing copper oxide or silver nitrate respectively, with a post-firing reduction in sawdust. Height of tallest piece 51 cm (20 in). By DIETER BALZER (West Germany), 1986. (Photo: Udo Hesse)

Stoneware bottle, wheel-thrown in sections. A small amount of clay stained with oxides has produced the natural throwing spiral of darker material visible beneath the glaze. Height 26 cm (10¼ in). By LUCIE RIE (UK).

Composite earthenware bowl form made in three sections which slot together. Partly decorated with a matt, lead bisilicate glaze, and burnished where unglazed. Diameter 58 cm (23 in). By LOUISE GILBERT SCOTT (UK), 1986. (Photo: Warwick Sweeney)

Thrown stoneware bowl. The form is distorted and is filled with inlaid white and coloured strips of T-material. Diameter 30.5 cm (12 in). By GLYNN HUGO (UK).

For several years **Louise Gilbert Scott** (UK) has been fascinated by the moving shapes of the fairground, and by spinning tops and discs which create different planes through their movement. Many of the pots she has made reflect this interest in the way that they tend to lean and tilt from a central point. Certainly, her distinctive bowl shapes evolved unintentionally during her study of these phenomena. Her initial idea was to attempt to describe movement within a pot that had been prepared from a flat disc pressed into a simple, conical bowl form. She found this form ideal for developing variations on a theme, while providing a good surface for decoration. Eventually, her ideas moved on and she began to use single press-moulded rings of clay stacked one on top of the other, rather like the neck jewellery worn by the Masai women of Africa. In this she was partly influenced by the limitations imposed by the materials and by the size of her kiln. She experienced difficulty in building some of the bowl shapes in one piece without losing several through cracking and warping, so she began to make separate rings to be assembled *after* firing. This opened up fresh possibilities of scale and versatility of form, and she now finds herself *beginning* the exploration of new ideas with separate pieces in mind. Most of the work is done in a grogged, red earthenware clay, painted and burnished with coloured slips. These are bisque-fired, supported in setters to prevent distortion, to between 1120°C and 1140°C to achieve a richer clay colour. Transparent and coloured glazes are applied later, fired to 1060°C.

These circular bowls present clean, crisp profiles to the viewer. Some rest on the sharp point of an inverted cone tilted until the outer edge makes

contact with the supporting surface and provides stability. Others stand precariously on three points of a curved, triangular shape, the centre of which has been cut out to receive the conical base. Broad, pressed rings attached to the open rim of the cone offer a wide expanse of smooth clay that invites decorative treatment.

The slip-cast forms by **Leo King** (New Zealand) also have the appearance of bowls, but he admits to having little interest in what happens below the wide rims which carry his crisp, linear designs. His conception is of a flat plane supported in space, and he is concerned mainly with the two-dimensional exploration of linear elements which relate both to the periphery and to the 'central' well of the vessel, illustrated here. For him, that hollow within the plane suggests infinity.

The circle, with its inherent symbolism of harmony and perfection, does not impose the sort of limitations on the linear drawing that might be encountered with other shapes. On a practical level also, the circular form and round hole are less subject to accumulated stress and consequent failure when thinly cast porcelain sheets are used. King believes the discipline of slip casting to be important to him, while the speed and accuracy of production, allied to the cleanliness of the cast surface, allows him to retain full control of the design. This form is assembled from three separate pieces before once-firing in an oxidizing atmosphere to 1240°C. After firing it is polished and left unglazed except for the interior well, which is either glazed black or painted with a metallic oxide mixture of manganese and copper.

Earthenware bowl form made in three press-moulded pieces, bisqued to 1120°C and glazed at 1060°C, with metallic black glaze and white enamelled lines. Diameter 46 cm (18 in). By LOUISE GILBERT SCOTT (UK), 1985. (Photo: Karen Norquay)

Slip-cast porcelain vessel with incised linear marking filled with dark-stained slip. The hollow section is painted with a combination of manganese and copper oxides to produce a bronze, lustrous surface. Fired to 1240°C in an oxidizing atmosphere. Diameter 37 cm (14½ in). By LEO KING (New Zealand), 1985.

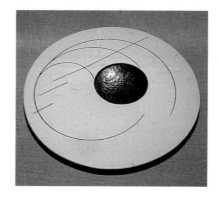

Right: Composite bowl form, unglazed porcelain, with free-standing, balanced assembly of four hemispherical shapes coated with oxides. By LEO KING (New Zealand), 1981.

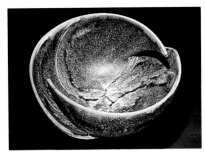

Hand-built porcelain bowl form with cut sections and cobalt/rutile glaze. By INGVIL HAVREVOLD (Norway), 1985. (Photo: Teigens Fotoatelier)

The work of some seventeenth-century engravers as well as that of the English artist Ben Nicholson has also had a particular influence on Leo King. Their use of varying thicknesses of line and geometric forms appeals to him. More especially, he feels indebted to Nicholson's 'circle and square' projects in white relief (1938), in which minimal colour was used. King uses a dark, stained slip to fill his incised linear designs, the composition of which must relate to the circular forms and create the illusion of movement.

A concern for abstract qualities is shared by many potters whose interest in functional attributes is secondary or even non-existent. **Judy Trim** (UK) endlessly refers to classical traditions, especially Cycladic, American

'Stars and Moon Bowl'. Coil-built piece in T-material fired to 1060°C, with metallic lustres decoration. Diameter 63.5 cm (25 in), height 23 cm (9 in). By JUDY TRIM (UK), 1985. (Photo: Leonard Hessing)

Indian and Egyptian work, in search of those qualities she describes as 'frozen music' or the 'still essence', but the pots she makes are mainly to do with how she *feels*. They belong to the contemplative as opposed to the functional. Above all, they are concerned with emotion. She expresses an affinity with Bernard Leach's statement that 'Potters are intensely aware of the inner nature of pots – that the inner comes before the outer – for it is inwardness and internal honesty that carries conviction.'

Many potters concentrate upon a specific theme or attempt to confine their work in some other way. Where materials and working methods are concerned, this approach allows them to become thoroughly familiar with the problems and possibilities involved. At the same time, they can develop ideas to greater depth. Judy Trim is certainly one such potter who enjoys working within a well-defined framework and, in particular, she welcomes the limitations imposed by using only two clays and firing no higher than 1060°C–1100°C. Pure T-material forms the body of many of her pots, all of which are coil built, and acts as a slightly coarse, white 'canvas' to support colour applied in the form of slips and metallic lustres. Red earthenware clay is used also for its 'warmth and gentle smoothness'. She prefers not to use glaze because she feels alienated by its hard stiffness; instead, surfaces are burnished and sometimes smoked in a sawdust kiln.

Her 'Stars and Moon' bowl is designed to be viewed well below eye level. Interest can then be focused upon the decoration and the broad, horizontal plane of the rim surrounding a central, inverted cone. The form rises sharply from a narrow base and widens rapidly to support this rim, which overlaps both the inner and outer surfaces of the wall. The form is thus constructed from two simple elements: a cone and a flat ring.

Jan Schachter (USA) sometimes uses coils or strips of clay woven together to produce small bowls or larger, dished platters. This is a method of construction that places the material under considerable stress during

An open-mesh bowl woven from coils of stoneware clay. Diameter 8 cm (3 in). By JAN SCHACHTER (USA), 1982.

Woven stoneware dish. The coils have been partially flattened by rolling and thus create greater visual interest. Maximum width 41 cm (16 in). By JAN SCHACHTER (USA), 1986. (Photo: Robert Aude)

Above: 'Wave Form' bottle. Brown-speckled stoneware. Height 43.5 cm (17⅛ in). By URSULA MORLEY-PRICE (France). (Photo: Westminster Gallery, Boston, USA)

Opposite above: Stoneware bowl, constructed from individually thrown units which have been cut and assembled by stacking one above the other. Oxidized firing to 1240°C in an electric kiln. Ridges formed by the prominent, overlapping joints suggest a feeling of flexibility, as if the form could continue to expand. Height 36 cm (14¼ in). By BEATE KUHN (West Germany), 1983. (Photo: Jochen Schade)

Opposite below left: Stoneware bowl, constructed from separate sections cut from thrown units. Oxidized firing to 1240°C in an electric kiln. Diameter 50 cm (19¾ in). By BEATE KUHN (West Germany), 1980. (Photo: Jochen Schade)

Opposite below right: Porcelain bowl with white glaze, constructed from eight small, open, wheel-thrown forms joined in radial formation. Reduction-fired to 1350°C in a gas kiln. Diameter 33 cm (13 in), height 9 cm (3½ in). By BEATE KUHN (West Germany), 1984. (Photo: Rolf Zwillsperger)

Right: 'Japanese Flange Pot'. Coil-built porcelain. Diameter 35.5 cm (14 in). By URSULA MORLEY-PRICE (France), 1985. (Photo: Denis Rigault)

the inevitable shrinking process, but it also offers unique possibilities for design due to its very limitations and therein lies its attraction.

Simple shapes and forms can be combined in countless ways to create more complex and unusual vessels. The work of **Beate Kuhn** (West Germany) has already been mentioned and illustrated in Chapter 2, but further examples from this innovative potter are worthy of examination. The bowl illustrated opposite (below left) is built from a number of separate sections of similar shape cut down vertically from thrown pieces. These have been joined edge to edge to produce a form reminiscent of cupped hands protecting the space within. Another, taller bowl (opposite above) consists of thrown and cut sections stacked one upon another. These are essentially semi-circular in shape and they gradually increase in size as they rise towards the rim to create deeply indented walls in the form of four lobes. The individual segments of all these vessels by Beate Kuhn have to be joined together with great care in order to ensure that the new form can withstand the stresses set up in drying and firing.

Forms built up from regularly repeated elements can suggest a feeling of movement or life. This is a familiar characteristic of nature which can be observed in plants, seashells and so on. It can also be achieved by adding or subtracting material, rhythmically, to or from the surface of virtually any simple vessel. **Ursula Morley-Price** (France), for example, creates rich visual interest in her hand-built bowl by pinching the rim into bold undulations which completely encircle the space within. This piece is made in porcelain and the thin, ruffled edges are picked out with a dark oxide for greater emphasis. The organic references are clear, but the translation into ceramic terms has been confidently achieved. The design has been developed to a point well beyond the mere imitation of nature.

The 'Wave Form' bottle by the same artist, on the other hand, is rather less satisfying, although similar rhythmic elements have been used. This form is fairly conventional in profile (as illustrated) and the wavy, vertical fins have been added merely as a decorative feature that bears little relation to the form itself. Where only two fins or wings are applied to opposing points on the circumference of a vessel its character is often altered more radically.

Porcelain bowl incised with leaf and flower design under a white, celadon-type glaze fired in reduction to cone 10 (1300°C). Height 13 cm (5 in). By ELAINE COLEMAN (USA), 1985. (Photo: Rick Paulson)

Tall porcelain vessel with lid, incised with an intricate design of leaves and flowers under a celadon glaze which becomes darker where it fills the incisions. Height 33 cm (13 in). By ELAINE COLEMAN (USA), 1985. (Photo: Rick Paulson)

When porcelain began to gain in popularity among studio potters in the late 1960s and 1970s it seemed that one of the most natural ways of using the material was to pinch and pull it between well-lubricated fingers into thin sheets, ribs or fins. Work by potters such as **Peter Simpson**, **Mary Rogers** and **Deirdre Burnett**, all of whom were working in England during that period, reached a high standard in both concept and craftsmanship. They created illusions of nature which were widely imitated, often crudely, by other, less-gifted potters, so that thousands of frilly, fungoid-like objects soon appeared in craft shops everywhere.

Porcelain also lends itself to extremely detailed work in modelling, carving and incising. Designs taken directly from plants, birds, animals and so on are often used to suggest vessel forms, but more frequently simple shapes are embellished with drawings, paintings or reliefs taken from such sources. Where these surface treatments encompass the whole form, rather than existing as isolated motifs, the effect is often one of greater unity. An example of a happy marriage between form and surface can be seen in the lidded porcelain pot by **Elaine Coleman** (USA). She has managed to incise a quite complex arrangement of leaves and flowers, suggesting growth and movement, which covers the surface completely but does not quarrel with the form. The bowl illustrated here, by the same artist, has a deeply cut rim and incised walls arising from the vertical growth pattern of the plant motif. Tinted, transparent glazes allow the precise drawing to show through clearly on both these pieces, accentuated where the glaze has pooled in the incised areas.

A similar glaze has been used over the carved iris design on the bottle vase by the Canadian potter **Harlan House**. In this case the drawing is simpler, with more of the pot left untouched, but the curvilinear pattern still manages to envelop the form.

Porcelain vessel with carved 'iris' decoration under a celadon glaze. Height 46 cm (18 in). By HARLAN HOUSE (Canada), 1986.

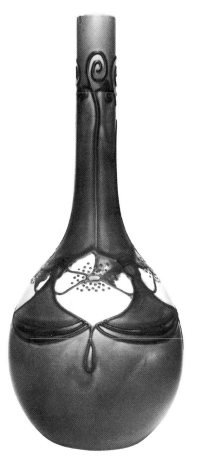

Far left: Earthenware bottle vase with tall neck and tube-lined relief decoration filled with coloured glazes. Made by Minton at Stoke-on-Trent, 1900–14.
(Photo: City Museum, Stoke-on-Trent)

Left: Tea canister in lead-glazed earthenware with green and yellow glazes. Made in Staffordshire in the mid-18th century.
(Photo: City Museum, Stoke-on-Trent)

More formal and stylized use of plant motifs can be seen in the eighteenth-century earthenware tea canister illustrated here, which was mould-made in Staffordshire. Its pineapple design is highlighted by runny glazes in yellow and green which leave no room for doubting the source of stimulus. An abstracted flower motif, picked out in relief by tube lining and coloured glazes, in the unmistakable style of Art Nouveau at the turn of this century, is illustrated by the earthenware bottle vase made by Minton. The design encircles the pot and extends almost to the top of its tall neck.

Below and below left: Stoneware bottle and bowl, both wheel-thrown, with linear designs incised through white glaze, fired to 1360°C in a reduction atmosphere. Height of bottle 25 cm (10 in), height of bowl 10 cm (4 in). By GOTLIND WEIGEL (West Germany), 1986. (Photos: E. Böhm)

'Misty Trees'. Porcelain bowl decorated with airbrushed ceramic stains and fired to cone 7 in an electric kiln. The surface has been polished with wet and dry silicon carbide papers. Diameter 21 cm (8¼ in). By PETER LANE (UK), 1986.

Undoubtedly, nature has always supplied the greatest stimulus of all. There is an immense range of natural forms and patterns from which to choose and adapt for the purposes of design. Although direct imitation of nature in ceramics has been popular at certain times, the more rewarding approach has always been to use nature only as a starting point. The smoothly rounded, tree-crested hills of the Berkshire Downs, which I knew so well as a boy, provided me with the stimulus for a series of porcelain bowls for several years. These featured hills and trees adapted within a carved and pierced design around the rims (see illustration on page 48). Exploration of this theme led to endless variations while keeping to the original bowl form. My enjoyment of undulating skylines, from the intimate lakeland fells of Cumbria (where I now live) to the awesome mountainscapes of the North American Rockies, prompted the development of many other carved rim designs. These eventually became abstracted to the point where the allusion to mountains was obscure, and 'waterfalls' were represented by no more than a vertical line of pierced holes.

Above: Porcelain vessel with lid and four lugs. Freely painted brushwork has been applied to the unfired glaze with mixtures of metallic oxides. The design has been softened as the glaze melted – and began to flow. Height 46 cm (18 in). By JOHN TAKEHARA (USA), 1985.

Hand-built porcelain vessel with wire-cut texture. By JOHANNES GEBHARDT (West Germany).

Tall stoneware vessel, thrown, and incised with a vigorous design of ravens which surround the form with flowing movement. Iron and manganese oxides provide the colours. Fired to cone 5. Height 51 cm (20 in). By FRANK BOYDEN (USA), 1985. (Photo: Jim Piper)

Stoneware platter with fluent drawing of 'fish bone' design. Unglazed and wood-fired. Diameter 61 cm (24 in). By FRANK BOYDEN (USA), 1985. (Photo: Jim Piper)

Frank Boyden (USA) is one artist whose love for life and for his immediate environment shines through his work. Living and working in his studio situated on rising land overlooking the Salmon River estuary on the beautiful Oregon coast of the United States is a constant source of inspiration for him. As a keen fisherman with a deeply felt concern for the ecology of the region, much of his work expresses aspects of the life cycle of the great salmon that come to spawn and to die in the upper reaches of the river. Large, thrown pots 'with a smooth surface and good form' are important to him for they provide the ideal background for his fluently incised drawings, executed with remarkable economy and boldness. The salmon figures prominently on tall vessels and wide platters. Boyden's recent work, in particular, has a good deal to do with the death of the salmon and with the scavenging ravens which feed upon them. This is an event he has often witnessed and which has influenced his thinking.

A different kind of figurative approach is demonstrated in the bowl by **Geoffrey Northcote** (UK). This was thrown with three horizontal flanges

Stoneware bowl, wheel-thrown, with a wood-ash glaze applied over iron oxide in the depressions. The 'accretion' decoration is neatly contained within the raised bands which were produced on the wheel. Diameter 30.5 cm (12 in). By GEOFFREY NORTHCOTE (UK), 1984.

spaced beneath the ledged rim and extending an equal distance from the main wall. The spaces between the flanges have been filled with recognizable seashore motifs, modelled in clay, to form an encircling, richly textured frieze. **Annette McCormick** (USA) takes realism a stage further in the fish stopper she has modelled to fit the top of her cone-shaped bottle, and in the more dramatic barracuda portrayed atop another tall bottle made in porcelain.

Some pots incorporating figurative elements appear to have literary associations or to suggest that their creator was at least prompted to express a story or hint at a hidden meaning or message. Narrative pieces illustrating a story through surface painting especially have a long and distinguished tradition. Greek earthenware vessels, from as long ago as the latter part of the seventh century BC, were richly adorned with pictorial elements. These were often scenes taken from the myths about the gods or the lives of heroes such as Heracles. They present us with an excellent picture of the everyday life, dress, culture and society of the time. Today, though, there are far fewer direct or figurative references made to religion by potters.

Occasionally, however, ambiguity adds to the interest of a piece. For example, **Jerry Rothman** (USA) has made a series of open vessel forms as sculptural objects that can also be classified as bowls. The viewer can read whatever he/she wishes into them. To some they will appear ritual-istic or descriptive, but there can be no doubt that they succeed as three-dimensional expressions in their own right and, however limited, as

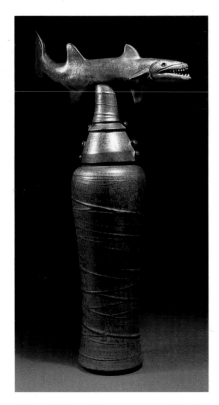

Above: Tall bottle form surmounted by a modelled stopper featuring a barracuda. This piece is made in porcelain clay with a raku firing to cone 03. Height 35.5 cm (14 in). By ANNETTE McCORMICK (USA), 1985.

Opposite above: Thrown bottle with stopper in the shape of a fish. The bottle has become a pedestal to support the modelled fish and its potential function as a container is thus disguised. Height 23 cm (9 in). By ANNETTE McCORMICK (USA), 1986.

Opposite below: Sculptural vessel form with human figure and two swans. Width approximately 56 cm (22 in). By JERRY ROTHMAN (USA).

functional vessels. In the piece illustrated a human figure in a semi-reclining position supports two swans so that the group, which partially and protectively encloses a volume of space forming a kind of bowl, presents us with a restful and evocative image.

Sometimes, individual pots are specifically designed to be seen together in a single group, and anyone who has physically arranged a display or exhibition will know that the way in which pots are placed in relation to each other can be quite critical. Altering the distance between them, even fractionally, seems to enhance or diminish their visual impact. Actually joining together a number of pots which are, themselves, individually complete offers many exciting possibilities. By combining several simple bottles into one piece, as illustrated, **Bruno** and **Ingeborg Asshoff** (West Germany) have created a striking group rather like a crowd of waiting and watching people. Similar bottle shapes could be arranged in a number of other ways also for a quite different effect.

Right: 'Family of Bottles'. Stoneware pieces, hand-built and fired to cone 6. Height 36 cm (14¼ in). By INGEBORG AND BRUNO ASSHOFF (West Germany), 1970. (Photo: Dagmar Grauel)

Above left: **Two thrown and turned bowl forms with various glazes and colours produced by copper oxide, fired in oxidation to cone 9 (1280°C). Height of tallest bowl 10 cm (4 in). By** GEOFFREY SWINDELL **(UK), 1985. (Photo: Bill Thomas)**

Above right: **Three bottle forms, wheel-made, each with a different combination of glazes. The colour is from copper oxide only, fired to cone 9 (1280°C). Height of tallest piece 14 cm (5½ in). By** GEOFFREY SWINDELL **(UK), 1985. (Photo: Bill Thomas)**

Stoneware bowl, wheel-thrown and mounted on a pedestal, with yellow engobe (burnished when leather-hard) and off-white feldspathic glaze. Fired in a reduction atmosphere to cone 8. Diameter 23 cm (9 in). By FRITZ ROSSMANN **(West Germany), 1985. (Photo: Foto-studio Baumann)**

Much of **Geoffrey Swindell**'s (UK) stimulus comes from the continuous thematic examination of thrown and turned bottle forms having unusual profiles with positive directional changes. Each piece is designed as a complete form in its own right, but visual interest is enhanced considerably when several variations of like forms are displayed alongside each other. This has become an aesthetic exercise, sustaining itself through the kind of enquiry which is open-ended and infinite. Different proportional relationships can be combined with accents of flanges and concave or convex curves varying in steepness and complexity, while colours and visual textures extend the range of possibilities even further. The pots illustrated are quite small in scale and are made with great precision and attention to detail. The one constant feature that is noticeable in most of Swindell's work is the relatively tall foot which elevates and displays the main body of the piece.

Any individual feature or element of design in three-dimensional form or surface treatment can be explored and developed through work on a series of pieces. **Gerald Weigel** (West Germany) has used a single linear accent in different ways on a number of slab-built, stoneware vessels. The basic forms he has made are simple in shape and profile. The surfaces are smooth and interrupted only by a line of contrasting colour, either inlaid or modelled in relief, running down the broadest face of the pot from top to bottom. Three of these pots are illustrated here and it is not difficult to imagine that there is considerable scope within this theme for the development of many other variations.

'Kastenform'. Slab-built, dark-stained stoneware with porcelain inlay fired to 1360°C in a reducing atmosphere. Height 20 cm (8 in). By GERALD WEIGEL (West Germany), 1986. (Photo: E. Böhm)

Below left: 'Flugelform'. Slab-built stoneware bottle with a rutile glaze reduction-fired to 1360°C. Height 38 cm (15 in). By GERALD WEIGEL (West Germany), 1983. (Photo: Jochen Schade)

Below right: 'Steinform mit Naht' (Stone Form with Suture). Slab-built stoneware reduction-fired to 1360°C. Height 30.5 cm (12 in). By GERALD WEIGEL (West Germany), 1985. (Photo: Jochen Schade)

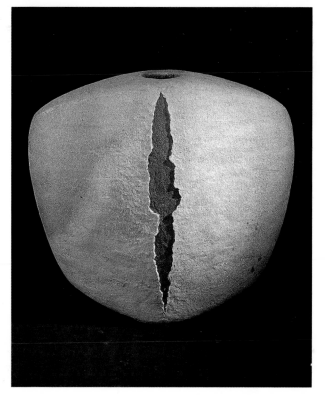

Limiting one's investigations like this can be very rewarding as it often opens up new horizons, especially when one is receptive to similar elements existing and waiting to be discovered in the immediate environment. For example, much of **Hans de Jong**'s (Holland) work is inspired by the shapes and patterns he sees around him in Holland. He has based many of his linear designs on patterns suggested by observing the layout of dykes and polders. These formal elements of finely drawn lines and rectangles are well suited to the forms he makes and they appear regularly in several aspects of his work.

The various qualities inherent in the clay itself supply more than enough stimulus for many potters, because the behaviour of clay bodies can differ widely according to their composition and the use to which they are put. Some kind of happy compromise must be achieved between the initial concept and what the properties of the material will allow. **Jeff Mincham** is an Australian potter who feels that the unusual properties of a buff raku body obtained from Queensland contribute a great deal to his ideas in his current work. This body is especially tolerant of some quite complex throwing techniques and accepts textural treatment very well. It can also withstand rough treatment in construction as well as sprayed slips when dry ('it is worth bringing it 2000 miles at considerable expense').

Bowl form, thrown in two parts. The major visual interest is in the unusually tall, split foot. Diameter 33 cm (13 in). By KAREN KARNES (USA), 1986.

Stoneware bowl with alternating layers of an ash and copper glaze giving variations in colour from light green to dark browns and blacks. Parts are covered with a feldspathic glaze stained with copper oxide. The 'decoration' is designed to intensify the feeling of space enclosed within the form, rather as the dykes and canals determine the landscape of a polder in the artist's home country. Diameter 30.5 cm (12 in). By HANS DE JONG (Holland), 1981.
(Photo: Cor Van Weele)

Below: Stoneware bowl with linear pattern scratched through black engobe, slab- and coil-built with coarse sculpture clay. Texture produced by scraping when dry. Fired to cone 6 with black glaze inside. Diameter approximately 38 cm (15 in). By LARRY ELSNER (USA), 1985. (Photo: Andrew M. Whitlock)

Double-walled raku bowl, wheel-thrown in one piece with hand-built additions. Sprayed with oxides and carbonates, fired to 1100°C (Orton cone 03), with post-firing reduction. Diameter 38 cm (15 in). By JEFF MINCHAM (Australia), 1985. (Photo: Grant Hancock)

Flask form, wheel-thrown in two halves and joined. The piece was then trimmed as a single unit with other components made by hand and added, together with a separately thrown neck. The form was bisqued to 900°C after the application of copper and lithium carbonates mixed with a small amount (5 per cent) of clear earthenware glaze, oversprayed with copper. Height 28 cm (11 in). By JEFF MINCHAM (Australia), 1986. (Photo: Grant Hancock)

Rolled and folded slab-built bowl in smoke-fired stoneware, with strong sculptural and textural interest. Diameter 28 cm (11 in). By YVETTE MINTZBERG (Canada), 1985.

Mincham's experience with raku firing prompted him to use this clay in an exploration of bowl forms where the inner and outer contours were in contradiction to each other. At first he joined together, one inside the other, two bowls of the same diameter but different depths, until he was able to devise a method of throwing the resulting form in one piece. The forming process is simple enough for a good thrower. He begins by making an even-walled sphere which is then closed off, trapping air inside. The surface is smoothed with metal shims and a hole made in the side near the base. Then various-shaped ribs are used to depress the top into a bowl form. If he seems to be losing control of the developing form, Mincham merely blocks the hole to retain the cushion of air within the sphere while adjustments are made. The process then continues as before until the desired shape is completed.

Through working in this way, Mincham has come to realize that some surfaces can extend his concept of form and that his use of certain additions can evoke quite a complex response from the viewer. But he never considers these elements in isolation because they are inseparable parts of the whole. He has now evolved a range of vessel forms which themselves promote further thought and stimulate new ideas. He refers to these forms as his 'ceramic alphabet'.

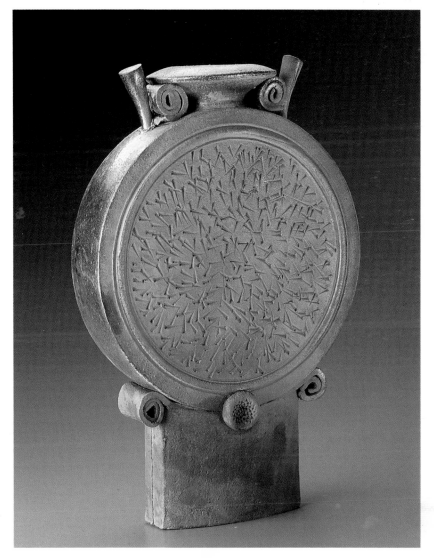

Porcelain bowl with rutile and copper oxide in a high zinc-barium-soda glaze. Fired in oxidation to cone 8. Diameter 10 cm (4 in). By SUE MEYER (South Africa), 1985. (Photo: John Peacock)

Opposite above left: Stoneware bottle, wheel-thrown with hand-built additions. The glazes, containing cobalt and iron oxides and having a crystalline character, are brushed on in two or three layers. Reduction-fired to 1310°C in a gas kiln. Height 32 cm (12½ in). By ERIK PLØEN (Norway), 1985. (Photo: Teigens Fotoatelier)

Opposite below: 'Bracelet Bowl'. Hand-built. By HENRY PIM (UK), 1985. In the Crafts Council Collection. (Photo: Tim Hill)

'Open Disk'. Stoneware vessel with tall, cylindrical foot. Moss-green glaze with melt fissures, sang iridescence and fire marks in reduction. Approximately 23×23×8 cm (9×9×3 in). By OTTO NATZLER (USA), 1985. (Photo: Gail Reynolds Natzler)

The development of a personal, visual language through the manipulation of form and surface often takes many years to establish. Pots made by hand tend to incorporate something of their maker's personality, although their creation will have been tempered by the level of skill and know-how available at the time they were produced. Interests and influences are rarely constant. Priorities alter so that aspects of life and ideas affecting work, which once seemed to be of over-riding importance, fade and are replaced by others. Sources of inspiration and the driving forces behind the work will always be as diverse as the individuals who produce it.

Above: **Stoneware bowl, hand-built, with glazes brushed on in layers, and colours obtained from cobalt and iron oxides. Fired in a reduction atmosphere to 1310°C in a gas kiln. Diameter 18 cm (7 in). By ERIK PLØEN (Norway), 1985. (Photo: Teigens Fotoatelier)**

4. DECORATION

'Decoration' is an unfortunate term when it comes to describing the surface treatment of ceramic forms since it has rather shallow connotations unsuitable for every situation. The word normally implies that decoration is something having a kind of separate identity, and indeed it is true that, in some cases, applied motifs may be completely unrelated to the underlying form. In such instances, their function is merely to prettify. (Many examples of this can be seen in industrially made tableware.) But, in the absence of any other more appropriate word, 'decoration' must also serve in reference to those design elements that contribute to a deeper union achieved between form, pattern, colour and texture. Wholesome and absolute integration of form and surface is the aim of most potters and they will all have their own preferred techniques which are designed to satisfy that end.

In general, the more simple the form, the greater complexity of pattern it will support, but the emphasis and placement of any pattern is of critical importance. A weak pot may be marginally improved by good decoration, but that which is poorly conceived or insensitively applied will spoil a good one. It is well known that alternating areas of colour or tone can play optical tricks on our powers of perception. The forms and profiles of ships, aircraft, vehicles and buildings were often disguised in this way during wartime. Equally, the marks we apply to the surfaces of pots contribute to (or detract from) their character, thus conditioning the viewer's response to them.

Opposite: Tea bowls, thrown and altered, in stoneware clay with multiple slips and glazes, fired in reduction to cone 11. These lively pieces have colours which appear to be suspended at different levels within the surface glaze. Glick says that he has to acknowledge the strong liking he has had for Oriental pots and he is indebted especially to the spirit of the casual, gestural motives found in the Shino and Oribe pots: in particular, the elaborately decorated box forms and asymmetrical tray forms, and the richly coloured, patterned surfaces associated with these wares. Diameter 10 cm (4 in). By JOHN GLICK (USA), 1985.

Below left: Stoneware vessel, thrown and turned, altered to an oval section, with stencilled glaze. Height 23 cm (9 in). By MONIKA SCHÖDEL-MULLER (West Germany), 1985. (Photo: Gertrud Glasgow)

Below: Porcelain bowl with a strong pattern of horizontal divided bands in a black matt feldspathic glaze. Diameter 20 cm (8 in). By HILDEGARD EGGEMANN (West Germany), 1985.

Right: 'Early Birds'. Stoneware vessels, coil-built upside down over a hump mould. The low-relief decoration of the birds was achieved by pressing the sharp edges of plaster fragments into the softened clay walls. After bisque firing, these bird motifs were washed with thin oxides and then wax-resisted before the matt black glaze was applied. The pots were fired in a top-loading electric kiln to cone 9 (for fourteen hours). Larger vessel 42×40× 15 cm (16⅜×15¾×6 in). By HIROE SWEN (Australia), 1985. (Photo: Cornel Swen)

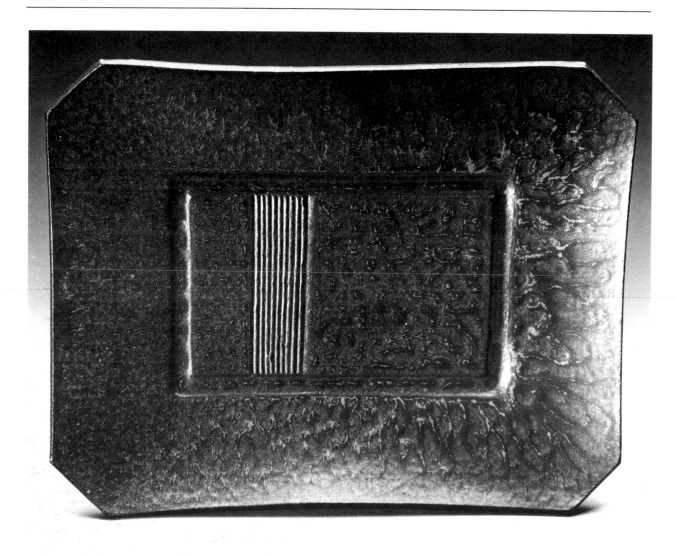

An interesting exercise is to take a simple, basic form (it could be a cylinder, a sphere, a rectangular box or a shallow dish) and to work out as many different ways as possible for treating the surface in order to complement and accentuate the form and, thereby, overcome its anonymity. One specific idea or theme can be explored to considerable depth through this activity. Although there can be no guarantee of success, the thought processes involved are certain to extend one's understanding and appreciation of that special relationship between form and surface. No rules exist that cannot be broken where design is concerned, but it is often helpful to begin by choosing some guidelines to follow. Working within some kind of framework, however restrictive that may seem at first, can produce the key to open up all sorts of creative opportunities.

Making just one incised line, a single brush stroke, an indentation or impressed mark, or the addition of a pellet of clay to the surface of a pot will immediately affect its character. A series of marks may be developed into an area of texture which can be set against plain, untouched or uninterrupted surfaces. The introduction of colour increases the options, and sometimes the problems, for the designer. Successfully organizing all these elements in terms of pattern, whether controlled in a consciously precise way, as in the style of some European potters, or in the freer manner of abstract expressionism, requires an intuitive awareness of form,

Pressed slab dish, stoneware, with dark, manganese glaze. The simple, but effective, geometry of the impressed centre section complements the almost metallic severity of the form, the surface of which is relieved by the textural nature of the glaze. Maximum width 30 cm (11¾ in). By JAN SCHACHTER (USA), 1986. (Photo: Robert Aude)

surface and spatial division. The word 'design' itself implies organization where options have been considered and decisions taken.

One of the most difficult decisions which I find has to be made is not so much where to start but when to finish. It is easy to fall into the trap of overworking an idea. What may appear to be a quite straightforward, visual statement is often harder to realize in practice.

Stoneware bottle form, fired to cone 7, with relief decoration. Height 38 cm (15 in). By INGEBORG AND BRUNO ASSHOFF (**West Germany**), 1985. (Photo: Bernd Kirtz)

Stoneware bowl, wheel-thrown, with orange and blue engobes (burnished when leather-hard), matt black glaze in parts, and off-white feldspathic glaze. Incised lines separate glazed and unglazed areas. The rim is accentuated by a sharp change in direction and colour. Fired in reduction to cone 8. Diameter 28 cm (11 in). By FRITZ ROSSMANN (**West Germany**), 1986. (Photo: Foto-studio Baumann)

Opposite: Porcelain bowl with celadon glaze, with an incised whiplash line. The rim and spots are burnished gold with cobalt and iron banding. Fired in reduction to cone 10 (1300°C). Diameter 10 cm (4 in). By DEREK CLARKSON (**UK**), 1985.

Shoji Hamada, the renowned Japanese potter and great friend of Bernard Leach, used the 'same' motifs on many of his pieces, although he treated each as a fresh expression and continuously refined the basic elements of the design. Most potters find that their forms or applied designs alter, sometimes imperceptibly, over a period of time, even though they may be pursuing a particular line of enquiry throughout. I have been surprised and stimulated, for example, to note the subtle changes that have taken place, unconsciously, over as short a period as two or three years in certain details of my own work. This is especially evident in the shifting emphases within proportional relationships and in the profiles of thrown porcelain bowls.

In this chapter we can examine a variety of techniques and some of the diverse approaches made by potters in the area of applied design. However, it is important to realize that techniques and working methods can serve as no more than the means by which ideas are developed and expressed. It also has to be acknowledged that potters can become so obsessed with the chemistry and technology of their craft that, in some cases, they come to rely too heavily upon those aspects and lose sight of all else.

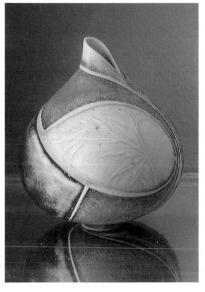

Above: Porcelain bottle with incised design and copper-red, copper-blue and celadon glazes fired in reduction to cone 12. Height 8 cm (3 in). By SCOTT MALCOLM (USA), 1985.

Slab-built, stoneware bottle with trailed glaze and brushwork decoration. Height 19 cm (7½ in). By SHOJI HAMADA (Japan).

Porcelain vessel with lid. The colour is produced with a 'fake' ash glaze applied thickly and thinly over wax resists, and dots of iron oxide/ash. Fired to cone 9 in reduction. 18×18 cm (7×7 in). By TOM TURNER (USA), 1985.

Processes, nevertheless, do provide many with the initial and ongoing stimulation. They can prompt the imagination and, sympathetically used, can offer opportunities for intensely personal aesthetic exploration in ceramic terms. But that human element of feeling and individual response to experience should always remain indispensable ingredients, and the following sections should be read with this understanding in mind. Like many other potters, I am happy to describe the way I think and work. I also freely explain the techniques I employ because they are no more than adaptations of age-old methods adjusted to my own personal needs. More importantly, they provide me with a kind of 'vocabulary' which, like all others, can be used by anyone else in various and divergent ways to express totally different ideas.

Greek oil bottle, h. 24 cm (9½ in), *c.* 6th C BC.

Persian vase, h. 34.5 cm (13⅝ in), 12th C.

Designs that fit the form

Dishes or shallow bowls present fewer problems for decoration than most taller vessels because although they have two distinct sides only one is normally visible to any large extent. This can be read and understood at a glance, for any design applied to that upper surface is framed and contained by the rim or outer edges of the piece. Artificial boundaries, usually in the form of horizontal bands or as vertical lines dividing a pot into vertical segments, can also be used to separate areas of the design. This device helps to give the most complicated combination of patterns some degree of stability and also aids comprehension. Examples of this can be seen in pots from many different cultures. Some of the most notable of these were produced in ancient Greece where vase painting was developed to a high art. Horizontal banding not only provided a firm base line to support pictorial subject matter but also helped to accentuate aspects of the three-dimensional form.

A bottle lends itself to this kind of framework easily, with divisions being made at one or more natural points such as the lip, the junctions of neck and shoulder or shoulder and body, below the belly or near the foot. Similar divisions appear natural and will often succeed when proportionately applied to a tall cylinder as well. Again, this underlines the direct relationship to human scale. Painted or incised bands are especially useful in marking out manageable areas for decorative treatment on an otherwise smooth form having no definite changes in profile. They can also be used, of course, as decorative features in their own right.

Where a vessel does have positive directional changes in its form these can serve in the same way as added bands because they can be used as points at which to start or end applied designs. Often the change will be emphasized by an area of texture or a difference in colour or tone. The porcelain bottle decorated with painted gold lustre by **Mary Rich** (UK) illustrates a happy marriage of form and decoration by confining the pattern between two such changes in the profile. The geometric nature of the pattern also helps to tie those points together. The bowl by **Judy Trim** (UK) has small squares and triangles of painted lustres arranged in bands around the broad inner rim, forming a frame of concentric circles: a simple but effective design.

Right: Porcelain bottle with a semi-opaque glaze over pale cobalt wash. Fired to cone 10 (1300°C) with gold and copper lustre decoration. Height 13 cm (5 in). By MARY RICH (UK), 1985.
(Photo: Matthew Donaldson)

Opposite: Porcelain bowl, thrown and carved, unglazed. Diameter 13 cm (5 in). By SANDRA BLACK (Australia), 1984.
(Photo: Peter Lane)

Below: 'Summer Sun Bowl'. Coil-built piece in T-material fired to 1060°C, with decoration in coloured slips and metallic lustres. Diameter 63.5 cm (25 in), height 25 cm (10 in). By JUDY TRIM (UK), 1986.
(Photo: Leonard Hessing)

Another use of banded lustres is shown in the bowl by **Vic Greenaway** (Australia), but in this instance sharply drawn lines of different widths near the rim prepare the eye for the top edge curving over and partially enclosing the inner space. They are rather like the metal hoops of a wooden barrel and add to the visual tautness of the form. The freer brushwork motif lower down the wall appears to be tightly held in suspension by the thin horizontal bands encircling the widest point of the bowl. The burnished bowl by **Robyn Stewart** (New Zealand) also has a banded upper section, but, although the incised lines have been drawn with equal precision, the sense of tension is reduced by the curling motif which overlaps the bands.

Deep bowl form, thrown in white semi-vitreous stoneware using Australian kaolin and ball clays. Decorated in a wash of cobalt and iron with bronze and platinum lustre additions. Fired in reduction to 1300°C. The glaze is a high magnesium matt (with added red terracotta clay to give slight speckle and tonal variation towards the top). This is a simple, classical shape tightly controlled in the throwing and in the precise placement of horizontal bands. The severity of the form has been softened by the delicate, spontaneous brushwork of the motif. Diameter 30.5 cm (12 in). By VIC GREENAWAY (**Australia**), 1985. (Photo: Ray Kinnane)

Coil-built bowl, burnished, with carved linear decoration and low-fired in a mixture of dung, leaves and wood chips for approximately twenty-four hours. The carved design owes something to the potter's Celtic origins as well as to the Maori patterns to be found in New Zealand. 38×18 cm (15×7 in). By ROBYN STEWART (**New Zealand**), 1985. (Photo: Howard Williams)

Above: Earthenware press-moulded bowl. The pattern is painted with commercially produced lustre glazes and metal lustres in combination. Width 51 cm (20 in). By PETER MOSS (UK), 1985.

Bowl form constructed from two press-moulded pieces (T-material), bisqued to 1120°C and glazed at 1060°C, with a black metallic glaze and coloured enamel stripes. Diameter 38 cm (15 in). By LOUISE GILBERT SCOTT (UK), 1985.
(Photo: Karen Norquay)

This notion of taut compression is explored in a different way by **Tom Coleman** (USA) and **Horst Kerstan** (West Germany). In the case of **Coleman**'s pot it is as if a piece of string had been tightened around an inflated form which offered some resistance to the external pressure. Placing this feature above the centre line creates a more interesting image. **Kerstan**, on the other hand, bands his bowl approximately halfway up the wall, but draws attention to the softness of the material with further, rapidly made, indented marks breaking across the horizontal line. A rather more clinical approach to the banded division of vessel forms can be seen in the crisply thrown pieces by **Ursula Scheid** of West Germany. In the bowl illustrated here she makes excellent use of unglazed bands to achieve strong tonal contrasts.

The division and subdivision of a pottery surface into areas of pattern, texture, tone or colour can be made as simple or as complicated as best suits the form and the potter, but whatever the final result, the success and acceptability of the piece will be partly dependent on individual tastes. If a group of experienced potters were each given exactly the same vessel form with absolute freedom to choose and apply to it whatever they believed to be the most suitable surface treatment (not necessarily pattern), there would be an abundance of different answers to the same problem.

Opposite above left: Cylindrical porcelain bowl, partly banded with iron slip, and polished where unglazed. Fired in reduction to 1360°C in a gas kiln. Diameter 13 cm (5 in). By URSULA SCHEID (West Germany), 1980. (Photo: Bernd P. Göbbels)

Opposite below: Double mound vessel, wheel-thrown, with straw and rice hull ash glaze sprayed over iron-bearing slip, fired in reduction to cone 10. Diameter 33 cm (13 in). By TOM COLEMAN (USA), 1985. (Photo: Rick Paulson)

Below: Bottle form, stoneware, with different layers of an ash glaze stained with iron oxide, partly covered with a feldspathic glaze containing cobalt. The use of straight lines on the surface of so many of de Jong's pieces reflects the mathematical precision of the drainage dykes and canals of his native country. Height 38 cm (15 in). By HANS DE JONG (Holland), 1982. (Photo: Cor Van Weele)

Above: Stoneware bowl, wood-fired, with textural interest from the effects of flying wood ash. This piece retains evidence of the soft condition of the clay when vigorously incised. Diameter 13 cm (5 in). By HORST KERSTAN (West Germany).

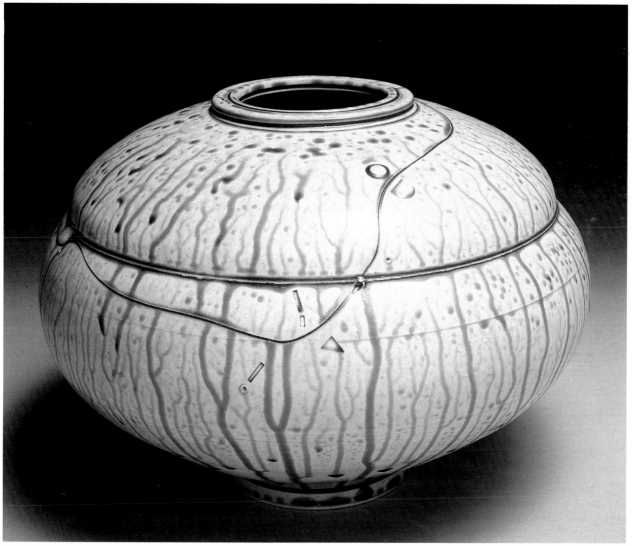

Porcelain vessel, thrown and carved with a
pattern (inspired by elements of natural
design and the movement of water) under a
celadon glaze. By ANNE-MARIE BACKER MOHR
(Norway), 1985.
(Photo: Teigens Fotoatelier)

Carved and incised decoration

The slightest unintentional nick in the rim of a fine porcelain bowl
interrupts the line in an uncomfortable way, but a series of them, regularly
placed, immediately seems to suggest a foliated form. This is a simple
device which was eloquently used by Chinese potters of the Sung period
(960–1279). More extravagant cuts intruding deeper into any rim will
lead the eye down the wall and exert additional influence on the elevation.
However, fired to maturing temperature, an open porcelain form such as a
bowl will be weakened physically by the removal of large areas of clay
from the wall, especially where the cuts are near-vertical. The risk of
distortion can be reduced if similar quantities of material are cut away in
the form of a multitude of relatively small holes, leaving the main fabric of
the wall intact as a kind of fretwork pattern. This method of decoration is
well illustrated in some Oriental porcelains and in the beautiful pierced
earthenware vessels from sixteenth- and seventeenth-century Persia.

Porcelain vessel incised with a leaf design under a white celadon-type glaze. Height 35.5 cm (14 in). By ELAINE COLEMAN (USA), 1985. (Photo: Rick Paulson)

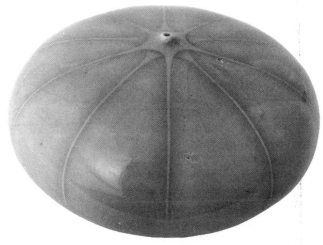

Porcelain form with carved design under a celadon glaze fired in reduction to cone 12. Diameter 10 cm (4 in). By SCOTT MALCOLM (USA), 1985.

Porcelain bowl, with incised decoration made with a fine needle, glazed with 'manganese gold' and fired to 1260°C in oxidation. Height 35.5 cm (14 in). By PETER BEARD (UK), 1985.

Below right: Burnished vessel, wheel-thrown, with carved pattern and spots of gold-leaf decoration. Height 35.5 cm (14 in). By PETRUS SPRONK (Australia), 1985.

Below: Open vessel form with burnished surface and carved linear pattern. By PETRUS SPRONK (Australia), 1985. (Photo: Michael Kluvanek)

Cutting, carving, incising and piercing into and through the walls of ceramic vessels is part of a very long tradition of decorated wares. Double-walled pieces, too, were often produced so that the most intricate network of pattern could be cut through the outer wall without restricting the functional possibilities of the vessel. Sometimes, a glaze that was designed to melt and flow was used to fill the holes with transparent colour, preserving the options of function without obscuring the pattern. In such a case the glaze increases the strength and durability of the vessel. Yet glazes are by no means essential to function or decoration, and some potters spurn their use altogether.

White, carved surfaces respond well to light passing across and, in the case of translucent bodies, right through them. Both bone china and porcelain have been widely used in this way by many studio potters who have found inspiration in the technique of carving itself.

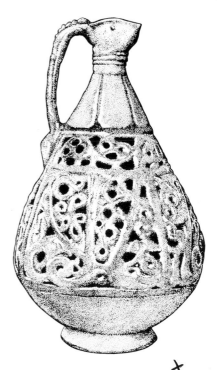

Persian ewer, h. 23 cm (9 in), 12th C.

Porcelain bowl, thrown and carved to reveal varying degrees of translucency. By ANNE-MARIE BACKER MOHR (Norway), 1986. (Photo: Teigens Fotoatelier)

Porcelain bottle vase with incised decoration under a celadon glaze fired in reduction to cone 10. By WALTER AND GISELA BAUMFALK (West Germany), 1986.

Porcelain bowl, wheel-thrown, turned,
carved and polished. Fired to cone 9 in
an electric kiln. Diameter 10 cm (4 in).
By SANDRA BLACK (**Australia**), 1985.
(**Photo: John Austin**)

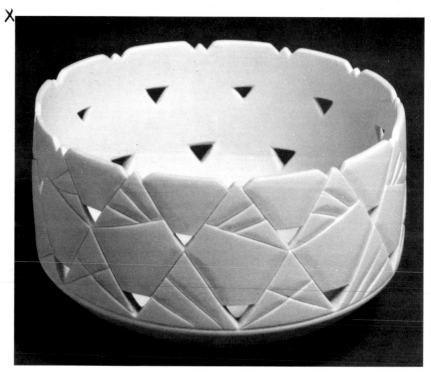

Contemporary trends in design, architecture, interior decoration,
fabrics, dress fashions, jewellery, painting and sculpture have provided the
Australian potter **Sandra Black** with a wealth of ideas for her finely carved
porcelain and bone china bowls. There is more than a hint of Art Deco in
her work and she also expresses interest in the work of artists like Escher.
In many of her pieces she makes use of positive changes of plane or
directional movements in the profile; these become the natural boundaries
for surface carving. Patterns consisting of straight, diagonal lines are cut
boldly into the surface of leather-hard porcelain clay with a sharp surgical
knife. Lines which meet at opposing angles are carefully carved to create
the impression that they pass under or over one another. Incisions are
made into the wall up to a depth of half its thickness, which is
approximately 2 mm ($\frac{1}{12}$ in). In some places the wall is pierced and cut
away altogether. The interiors of these bowls are not decorated, but
openings in the wall, forming part of the carved design, are tidied up and
smoothed to reduce the severity of the cut edges. Rims, too, are often cut in
an ordered, rhythmic way to accommodate patterns extending up the face
of the wall. Such designs draw attention to the perimeter or final edge of
the piece with a band of pattern that surrounds and frames the space
contained within.

Deep bowl shapes which curve upwards to present a smooth, broad
expanse of vertical wall are the perfect vehicles for **Angela Verdon**'s (UK)
delicately reticulated patterns. She works in bone china, a difficult material
to control and manipulate. She slip-casts her basic form very thinly and
fires it to a low bisque before commencing any decorative carving, because
in the green, unfired, and extremely fragile state such intricate treatment
would be impossible. The edges of the piece are ground and sanded before
she begins working into and through the surface with a dentist's drill.
Coloured stains are sometimes applied to the incised marks for greater
emphasis. The bowl is then fired to Orton cone 6 and soaked at that
temperature for two hours. Finally, the bowl is polished with a wet and
dry Carborundum paper.

Bowl, slip-cast in bone china, with pierced and semi-pierced band and burnished finish. By ANGELA VERDON (UK), 1982. (Photo: John Coles)

Below: Bowl, slip-cast in bone china with pierced decoration. Fired to 1220°C (cone 6) and finally burnished. Diameter 9 cm (3½ in). By ANGELA VERDON (UK), 1984. (Photo: John Coles)

Carved areas, especially in porcelain or bone china, can be made very smooth to the touch by polishing them with an abrasive paper coated with fine grades of silicon carbide grit. The advantage of this method is that it renders glaze, which might otherwise reduce the sharpness of the design, unnecessary. It is possible to use the same finishing treatment, in the interests of clarity, on other high-fired pieces decorated with oxides or ceramic stains. The colours will retain their full brightness without being softened or obscured by glaze.

Bowls, or other vessel forms, fired at lower temperatures are more capable of surviving the stress set up by those long continuous cuts that would lead to collapse or severe distortion if fired higher. Porcelain bodies, often fired well below the point of maturation, are preferred for their whiteness by a number of modern potters who have no need or concern for functional requirements. This gives them the essential freedom they want to explore combinations of form and pattern which otherwise might be impossible. Opportunities then open up for a radical reassessment of the bowl as a medium of expression unhindered by the demands of the material itself.

Right: Porcelain bowl, press-moulded from rolled slabs with inlaid black squares. The relief pattern of lines forms rectangles to enclose the squares under a transparent, matt glaze. Fired in reduction to cone 10. Diameter 23 cm (9 in). By ALINE FAVRE (Switzerland), 1985.

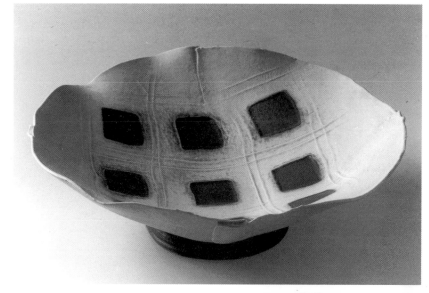

Opposite above: Thrown and cut bottle form. By LLUIS CASTALDO (Spain), 1986.

Opposite below: 'Fragments of Bowls'. Wheel-thrown porcelain, with cut and sawn rims, burnished and polished, fired to cone 9. By HORST GÖBBELS (West Germany). (Photo: Uellendahl)

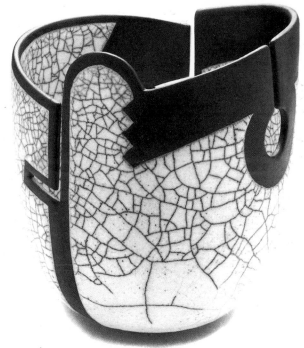

Gary Wornell (UK), using a porcelain body, has produced some adventurous low-fired pieces, simple in shape, with vibrant pattern based on the interplay of contrasts between black and white. All his bowls are thrown and trimmed to achieve an even wall thickness, almost as if the pot had been cast in slip but without the limitations that that method would have placed on the development of subtle variations in profile and proportion from one piece to another. Designs are drawn directly onto the pots, using templates made from old, plastic drum heads which bend to the curvature of the wall. A sharp scalpel is then used to cut out these stencilled shapes from the wall. After sponging the burred, cut edges, small plastic clamps are carefully positioned to hold in place the sides of any deep cuts (which are likely to separate further while drying). During bisque firing, these plastic clamps are replaced by high-bisqued ones in order to minimize the risk of warping.

Bowl with low-fired porcelain body and cut-away sections. Latex-resist decoration where black, and white crackled glaze, fired to 900°C in an electric kiln and reduced (raku fashion) in sawdust when removed hot from the kiln. The black areas have been darkened with an application of a shellac solution. Diameter 15 cm (6 in). By GARY WORNELL (UK), 1985. (Photo: Peter Lane)

Following the bisque fire, patterns are redrawn onto the pots, using plastic templates, to harmonize with the cut-away elements and create a kind of visual balance. This bold surface treatment complements the equally positive, pierced patterns confidently cut through the thin walls. Before dipping the bowls in glaze, latex resist is painted on to protect unglazed areas which are later blackened in a fast, raku-type firing. This is conducted to 900°C in a top-loading electric kiln with one piece at a time. Flat-bottomed pieces are protected from thermal shock by firing them on a cold stilt placed on the kiln shelf immediately beforehand; otherwise cracking would occur with the sudden, direct transfer of heat from the hot shelf to the base of the pot. The firing cycle takes about twenty minutes. A black shellac solution is later painted on and burnished into the unglazed parts of the design in order to heighten the contrast of black against white.

Porcelain bodies fired to such low temperatures have little strength and the pots must be handled with special care or they will break easily. Despite this disadvantage, they do offer particular options in surface treatment and in colour response unmatched by other light-coloured bodies; and although the fragility and porosity of pots made from this low-fired porcelain body preclude their use as containers for liquids, this is more than compensated by their decorative function.

Bowl with low-fired porcelain body, thrown and turned, with cut-away sections. Latex-resist decoration where black, and white crackled glaze, fired to 900°C in an electric kiln and reduced (raku fashion) in sawdust when removed hot from the kiln. The black areas have been darkened with an application of a shellac solution. Diameter 18 cm (7 in). By GARY WORNELL (UK), 1985.

Bottle form, thrown and altered, with incised decoration and painted slips and stains. Low salt-fired. Height 16 cm (6¼ in). By GRETE NASH (Norway), 1984. (Photo: Kjartan Bjelland)

Porcelain bowl with black slip and laminated coloured inlay design rolled into applied sheet. Unglazed and fired to cone 10 (1300°C) in an electric kiln. Height 13 cm (5 in). By GARY WORNELL (UK), 1985.

It is possible to carve stoneware and earthenware bodies, too, but their composition is usually more granular, which can prohibit work involving fine detail. Even so, the West German potter **Horst Göbbels** has produced an exciting series of exquisitely carved, incised and pierced bowls (see illustration). Strong diagonal lines, scored into the concave upper surface, sweep up to the sharp, partially eroded peaks forming a jagged top edge. This wheel-thrown vessel was painted with iron oxide (Fe_2O_3) to clothe it in a single, dark colour, and then reduction-fired in a gas kiln.

This rhythmic repetition of diagonal lines suggests a feeling of rotational movement and the phenomenon is illustrated further in bowls by **Derek Clarkson** (UK), **Robin Hopper** (Canada), **Ulfert Hillers** (West Germany)

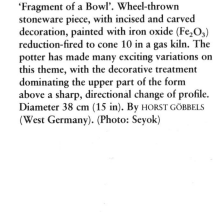

'Fragment of a Bowl'. Wheel-thrown stoneware piece, with incised and carved decoration, painted with iron oxide (Fe_2O_3) reduction-fired to cone 10 in a gas kiln. The potter has made many exciting variations on this theme, with the decorative treatment dominating the upper part of the form above a sharp, directional change of profile. Diameter 38 cm (15 in). By HORST GÖBBELS (West Germany). (Photo: Seyok)

Raku bowl, thrown and turned, banded with copper oxide, with porcelain body slip painted on in diagonal stripes. The soft, alkaline glaze has been reduced by plunging the bowl in sawdust when taken hot from the kiln. Diameter 17 cm (6¾ in). By DEREK CLARKSON (UK), 1985.

Deep agate-ware bowl in three colours. The diagonal fluting has exposed the coloured layers within the wall of this thrown vessel, while the spiral movement of colour across the flutes has been produced by raising the wall during throwing of the initial cylinder. Height 20 cm (8 in). By ROBIN HOPPER (Canada), 1980.

Below: Stoneware bowl with incised diagonal lines and brushed glazes. By ULFERT HILLERS (West Germany), 1986.

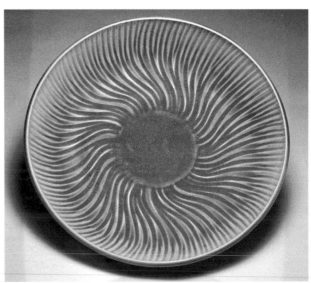

and **Karl Scheid** (West Germany). I have used a similar movement myself on the inside of a shallow bowl, carved with a wire loop while the clay was in a leather-hard condition. The satin-matt glaze is thinner on the ridges left by the carving so that the porcelain body shines through to give greater accent to the swirling pattern. The tall bottle vases by **Chris Staley** (USA) also have deep, freely cut faceted surfaces which leave no room to doubt the soft condition of the clay when worked upon.

Above: Shallow porcelain bowl, wheel-thrown and carved with a spiral pattern under a satin-matt green glaze which has gathered more thickly in the depressions to accentuate the design. Fired in an electric kiln to cone 9. Diameter 38 cm (15 in). By PETER LANE (UK), 1985.

Above left: Porcelain bowl with diagonal fluting. Copper slip was painted on the outside prior to carving the flutes. The white feldspathic glaze has been coloured red by the copper in reduction to 1360°C. Diameter 11 cm (4½ in). By KARL SCHEID (West Germany), 1984. (Photo: Bernd P. Göbbels)

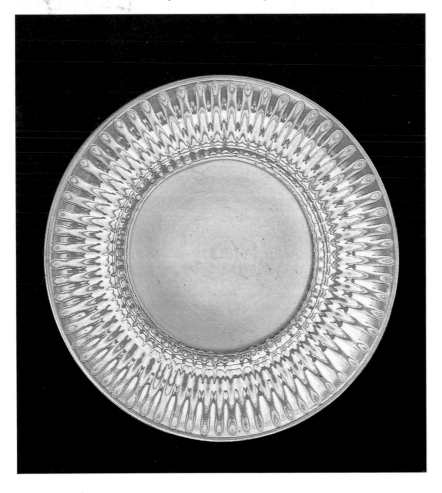

'Feather Basket Bowl'. Agate porcelain piece, thrown in two parts. Fluting has revealed the different coloured clays and produced a strong pattern. The form was inspired by Northwest Coast Indian basketry. Fired in oxidation to cone 9. Diameter 35.5 cm (14 in). By ROBIN HOPPER (Canada).

Stoneware vessel, thrown and turned, altered to an oval shape and sprayed with a light green slip. The pattern has been achieved by spraying a black, semi-matt glaze over a stencil. Fired in an electric kiln to cone 9. Height 26 cm (10¼ in). By MONIKA SCHÖDEL-MULLER (West Germany), 1986.

Below: Bottle form with applied lugs. The deeply faceted body was cut when still damp and reveals the plastic qualities of the material. This vessel has been salt-fired with a copper-red glaze in reduction. Height 35.5 cm (14 in). By CHRIS STALEY (USA), 1985.

Porcelain bottle form, wood-fired, with faceted sides and applied lugs. Height 53 cm (21 in). By CHRIS STALEY (USA), 1986.

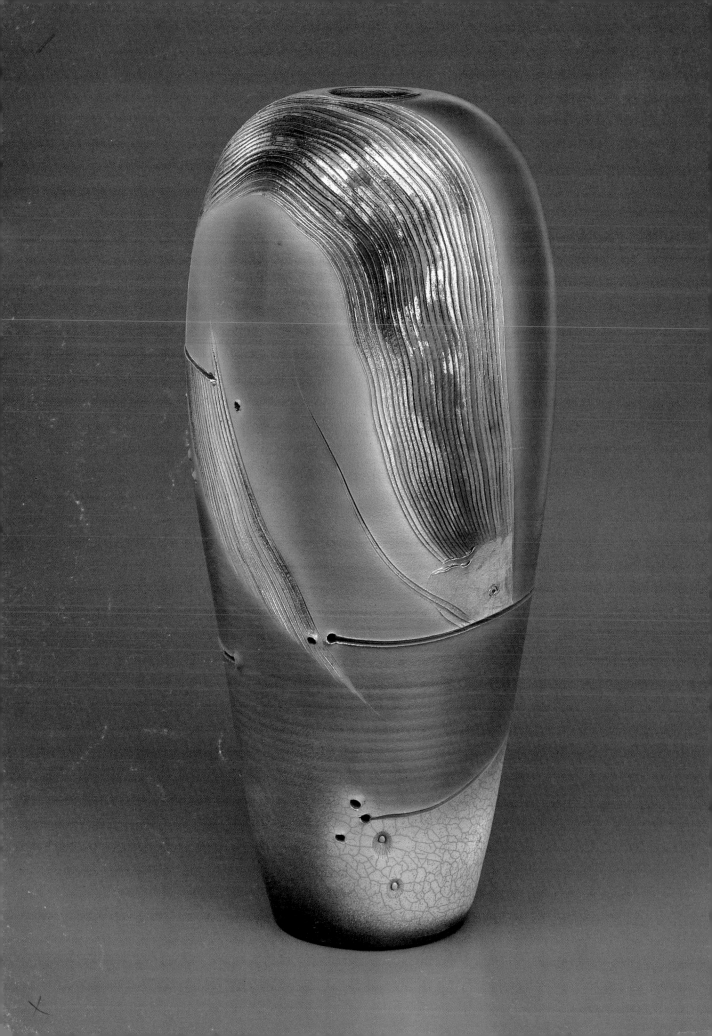

Porcelain bottle with incised pattern of plants under a green celadon glaze. Height 25 cm (10 in). By ELAINE COLEMAN (USA), 1985. (Photo: Rick Paulson)

Stoneware bottle forms with carved decoration, fired to cone 7. Height of taller piece 33 cm (13 in). By INGEBORG AND BRUNO ASSHOFF (West Germany), 1980. (Photo: Bernd Kirtz)

Opposite: 'Carp Vase'. Thrown and incised vessel, with polychrome terra sigillata and lustred glazes raku-fired in a sodium atmosphere to cone 04. Height 61 cm (24 in). By FRANK BOYDEN (USA), 1985. (Photo: Jim Piper)

Frank Boyden (USA), whose work was mentioned in Chapter 3, uses sharpened welding rods and engraving tools to attack the damp surface of his pots. 'The hardest thing to do is to make the first mark, but you have to start somewhere. You must defile the surface somehow. As soon as you have done that you've changed the entire piece. Things begin to evolve.' In the piece illustrated some of the incisions penetrate deeply, splitting the surface with expressive, curvilinear marks varying in intensity – thin to thick to thin. Again 'decoration' is an inadequate word to describe work that achieves, with strong feeling, such a close affinity between form and surface treatment. The character of the actual marks will vary according to the condition and resistance of the clay when they are made: if it is too wet the edges of scored lines will burr and if it is too dry the clay is likely to chip badly.

Another Oregon potter referred to earlier is **Elaine Coleman** (USA), who incises porcelain with flowing patterns derived from plants. Smooth shapes with clean, naturally curving profiles allow her drawings to clothe the forms completely. Transparent celadon glazes cover and fill the incisions, becoming darker in tone where the cuts are deep. Incised patterns under celadon-type glazes are part of a long tradition reaching back to the work of Chinese potters nine hundred years ago, but the technique is one which remains fresh and lively today when handled with such skill and sensitivity. The clay surface must be firmer than that required by Frank Boyden and, again, a confident, direct approach is important. Incisions can not be easily filled and the potter, once embarked on the process, must continue. The angle and depth of cut, together with the flow characteristics and colour of the glaze, will condition the final result. One way to ensure a crisp definition is to outline the design with a cut having one deep, vertical edge. Making a broader, angled cut which slopes down to meet this results in increasing the depth of the cut gradually and, thereby, the colour intensity of the glaze.

Thrown porcelain bowl with carved relief pattern under a light, feldspathic glaze, and copper-red glaze inside. Fired in reduction to 1360°C in a gas kiln. Height 8 cm (3 in). By KARL SCHEID (West Germany), 1981. (Photo: Bernd P. Göbbels)

Below: Slab-built porcelain vessel with satin-matt feldspathic glaze, blushed pink-red from the addition of copper oxide, reduction-fired to 1360°C in a gas kiln. The precise, rhythmic carving on this piece has been beautifully placed to complement and accentuate the whole form. 17×21×4 cm (6¾×8¼×1½ in). By KARL SCHEID (West Germany), 1983. (Photo: Jochen Schade)

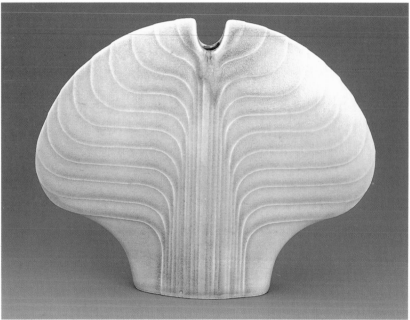

More abstracted, but equally precise, rhythmical patterns, carved in terraces engineered to catch the glaze, often appear in the work of the West German potter **Karl Scheid**. The directional flow of linear carving, as in the slab-built vessel illustrated, echoes and complements the form in a most harmonious way. Thinner glaze on the cut edges allows the white body colour to show through, outlining the design. This kind of surface treatment is fully integrated with the form in a way which transcends mere ornamentation; once again, words become inadequate before the object.

The plastic nature of clay is explored in a series of stoneware bottle forms by **Len Castle** from New Zealand. Here the wire-cut surface has suggested the form of his vessel. The linear patterns rippling across the surface are accentuated with a pigment made from burnt umber and manganese dioxide brushed into the grooves. Different thicknesses of tightly coiled wire can be used to provide these various movements and rhythms when it is pulled through a block of clay. Another method, employed by **Peter Beard** (UK), is to make lino cuts with swirling lines or geometric patterns which are then mounted on wood blocks for stamping designs into the damp clay. The changing levels thus produced serve to reflect the lustrous, metallic properties of the manganese-copper slip glaze with which he covers the surface.

Opposite: Hanging bottles, stoneware, with wire-cut decoration brushed with burnt umber and manganese dioxide. Heights: top left, 33 cm (13 in); top right, 21 cm (8¼ in); bottom, 28 cm (11 in). By LEN CASTLE (New Zealand), 1985. (Photos: Steve Rumsey)

'Fireworks'. Translucent porcelain bowl, incised and inlaid with multi-coloured porcelain slips, unglazed and polished with wet-and-dry silicon carbide papers. Fired in an electric kiln to cone 9. Diameter 23 cm (9 in). By PETER LANE (UK), 1985.

Hand-built porcelain bowl, unglazed, made from laminated slices of coloured clay in a zigzag pattern with pierced section. Fired in oxidation to cone 8 (1250°C). Diameter approximately 10 cm (4 in). By DOROTHY FEIBLEMAN (UK), 1984.
(Photo: Richard Ball)

Inlaid and laminated clays

Where clarity of pattern is an essential element, coloured clays, used in various ways, are extremely reliable. These can be used as slips, slurry, or in a plastic condition. They can fill incised lines with contrasting colours; they can be wedged together to create marbled areas and varying tones; or they can be inlaid for precise placement of coloured elements. Porcelains are especially suitable to be stained for this purpose because they can support a broad spectrum of pure, vibrant colours.

Stoneware bowl, made from a textured, imprinted slab and applied clay pieces. A round-bottomed cauldron was used as a former over which the slab was draped, and a foot was then added. Height 41 cm (16 in). By SANDY BROWN (UK), 1986.

The coloured material (of the consistency of very thick cream) can be blobbed into the incised areas so that it stands proud of the surface. As it dries it should be compressed a little with a thumbnail or a wooden tool. Another method is to apply the coloured clay in a slightly stiffer, plastic condition which enables it to be pre-shaped to fit broader prepared areas. The surface can be cleaned up, leaving the pattern clearly defined, by gently scraping with a flexible kidney-shaped steel palette and fine steel wool when completely dry.

Porcelain dished form constructed from coloured bodies laminated together. 34 cm (13½ in) square. By MARIAN GAUNCE (UK). (Photo: Karen Norquay)

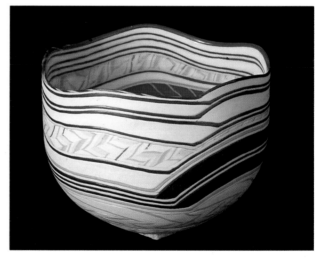

Extremely fine lines can be drawn into dry, or almost dry, clay. Colours in the form of prepared stains or oxides can then be brushed, sponged or rubbed into these marks, with any excess being removed so that the drawing becomes clearly visible. The reverse process of sgraffito drawing through colour-stained areas, or slips, or glazes, provides another equally direct way of decorating pots that is favoured by many potters. Some bowls by **Gerd Niort Petersen** from Denmark are beautifully conceived and executed using this method. The drawing is reserved, the colour minimal, and the effect delightfully refined.

Above: 'Pentagonal Blue'. Inlaid porcelain bowl (neriage technique), reduction-fired to cone 10. Diameter 21 cm (8¼ in). By HANS MUNCK ANDERSEN (**Denmark**). (**Photo: Mogens Gad**)

Above left: Stoneware bowl with decoration of inlaid coloured slips and gold leaf. Fired in oxidation to cone 10. By GERD NIORT PETERSEN (**Denmark**). (**Photo: Wolf Böwig**)

Opposite above: Porcelain bowls with incised linear design, reduction-fired to cone 10. Diameter 21 cm (8¼ in). By GERD NIORT PETERSEN (Denmark). (Photo: Mogens Gad)

Bottle constructed from inlaid sheets of coloured clay which has been cut and folded. Fired to cone 5, unglazed. Height 15 cm (6 in). By VIRGINIA CARTWRIGHT (USA), 1986. (Photo: Claire Henze)

Bowl, hand-built with coloured, laminated clays, cut, folded and joined, then fired to cone 5. The dark-glazed interior helps to concentrate interest on the flowing pattern of the outer surface. The irregular rim is a natural development of the folded sections. Diameter 28 cm (11 in). By VIRGINIA CARTWRIGHT (USA), 1985.

Perhaps the most interesting technique, which has been revived over the past few years, is that of laminating sheets of differently coloured clays and then using thin slices taken from across the 'grain' of the laminated slab to construct simple bowl forms. This method usually requires a plaster mould to support the form as it is built up from individual slices joined edge to edge with a little water or slip. Colours and patterns can be controlled with a degree of precision that few other methods can guarantee. A further bonus obtained with porcelain bodies is their translucency, which allows light to pass through the wall and 'mix' together any different colours applied to the inner and outer surfaces. Even with clay bodies lacking translucent properties, the patterns are interestingly mirrored on both sides of walls constructed from laminated slices.

This *nerikomi* technique (from the Japanese words meaning 'to mix' and 'to press into') is used very effectively by **Thomas Hoadley** (USA). He finds plenty of inspiration to sustain his work in the technique itself. There are various ways to make blocks of laminated clays, which have the pattern running right through the length as in a Swiss roll or certain fancy meats. Coloured clays are sliced and stacked repeatedly, resulting in a block or 'loaf' made up of thousands of overlapping layers. Cross-sectional slices taken from the end of the block will have the same pattern. Hoadley joins together several of these soft slices, stretching and shaping them freehand into bowl forms without the support of moulds. The laminated patterns are altered by the process of construction in a way that demonstrates the plastic nature of clay, with the many layers revealed as fine undulating lines embedded in a surrounding colour. The pattern thus becomes the substance and structure of the form itself, rather than merely a surface embellishment.

Among the most notable exponents of porcelain laminations in the form of bowls are **Curtis** and **Suzan Benzle** (USA) of Columbus, Ohio, and another American potter, **Dorothy Feibleman**, now working in London. The Benzles' work is not directly influenced by, or linked to, any particular style or period, although they do pay tribute to ceramic traditions 'that bridge the gap between aesthetics and human need'. Their work is concerned, primarily, with the surface treatment of form. They use porcelain, unglazed, for its pleasing tactile surface, its potential for colour, and its response to the infusion of light. Unusual bowls, shaped like melon

Above: *Nerikomi* vessel, hand-built with soft slices of multi-coloured porcelains joined together, stretched and shaped freehand, without the use of plaster moulds. Height 23 cm (9 in). **By** THOMAS HOADLEY (USA), 1986.

Above left: *Nerikomi* bowl, porcelain, hand-built with soft slices of multi-coloured laminated clays joined together without the use of plaster moulds. The vessel was then stretched and shaped, freehand, to reveal the soft, changeable nature of the material. 19×13 cm (7½×5 in). **By** THOMAS HOADLEY (USA), 1983.

Opposite: 'Tenderly'. Hand-built porcelain bowl constructed from coloured, inlaid sheets. Diameter 18 cm (7 in). **By** CURTIS AND SUZAN BENZLE (USA), 1984. (Photo: Curtis Benzle)

'Heartland'. Inlaid and rolled hand-built porcelain. The different coloured layers on the inner and outer surfaces of the thin translucent walls intermingle in a subtle way when light passes through them. 20×10× 43 cm (8×4×17 in). By CURTIS AND SUZAN BENZLE (USA). (Photo: Curtis Benzle)

slices or boats, balance on thin, upward-curving keels. When filled with light they appear at once both delicate and strong. Colours suffuse and glow within and without, blending and harmonizing throughout the form.

Dorothy Feibleman, also, is widely admired for her exquisite use of colour and pattern. She makes simple bowl forms with intricate, highly organized patterns constructed from thin slices of coloured porcelain laminated together. Her materials and the process she uses virtually dictate the way the decorative aspect of her work develops. This is because the patterns are formed by the structural process itself. She prefers to develop ideas without concern for domestic function and, although many of her bowls incline towards recognizably functional shapes, they can only serve as decorative pieces, to be cosseted and visually enjoyed. Among her most successful pieces are boat-shaped bowls which have coloured slices arranged horizontally in a linear design that follows and accentuates the form. Her love of minute detail sometimes extends to carving and piercing sections of a laminated bowl into a pattern of delicate tracery. Glaze is rarely used because she feels that it cheapens the appearance, since in order not to obscure the clarity of pattern she would have little option but to apply a glossy, transparent glaze.

Asymmetrical laminated porcelain bowl, with dark blue, green, turquoise, yellow and white stripes alternating with stripes of dots and circles. Length 10 cm (4 in). By DOROTHY FEIBLEMAN (UK). (Photo: David Cripps)

Porcelain bowl constructed from coloured bodies laminated together. This method enables precise placement of crisply defined coloured areas. Height 15 cm (6 in). By MARIAN GAUNCE (UK), 1986. (Photo: Karen Norquay)

Porcelain bowl, with blue and black thrown spiral pattern of laminated clays. Height 25 cm (10 in). By DOROTHY FEIBLEMAN (UK), 1985. (Photo: Richard Ball)

'Dreieckform mit Porzellan'. Triangular vessel form with porcelain inlay, partially glazed and reduction-fired to 1360°C. Height 23 cm (9 in). By GERALD WEIGEL (West Germany), 1985. (Photo: Jochen Schade)

Press-moulded stoneware dish, unglazed, made from laminated coloured clays stained with oxides. A range of tones has been achieved by intermixing light- and dark-stained bodies. Fired in oxidation. Width 41 cm (16 in). By MICHAEL BAYLEY (UK), 1985. (Photo: C. M. Dixon)

Stoneware clays tend to limit the brightness of colour due to traces of iron in even the lightest of them, but the particular character of stoneware bodies appeals to some potters far more than porcelain. **Michael Bayley** (UK) bases most of his work on two clay bodies, one light and the other dark. Intermixing these produces a range of different tones which he uses for his unglazed bowls and dishes. He describes his preference for bowls composed of laminated clays as 'forms to look into rather than at. There is

something mysterious, almost secretive about the inner face of a bowl. The outer rim conceals, in part, the inside. The inner form is rarely to be seen fully and thus is not instantly understood. In addition, it is subtly affected by light which illuminates the surface in unequal proportion, playing on the design as do clouds over hills. Because a bowl can be seen from so many different angles the relationship of design to shape is constantly changing. I enjoy the conflicting interplay this produces. The shape of the bowl and the design within appear to be opposing forces and I find the resolution of these always intriguing.'

Virginia Mitchem (USA) studied with Curtis Benzle in Columbus, Ohio, but chooses stoneware clays to make her large, laminated bowls. She begins by selecting a colour scheme and preparing stained clay bodies. These are carefully layered together in the form of a wedge-shaped block and then sliced into 1 cm (⅜ in) thick pieces. These are joined together with slip to form a large, circular slab which is rolled out to an even thickness and placed into a plaster 'slump' mould. These are simple, undulated cone-shaped moulds in the largest of which she leaves a space in the bottom so that she can push the finished greenware up from underneath away from the mould for easy removal. She finds that tipping these large moulds to release the bowl while balancing it at the same time is physically impossible for one person to manage. The form of any bowl can be adjusted slightly or altered radically after placing the slab into the mould either by lifting and stretching it (using rolled newspaper for supports) to create ripples, or by changing contours to enhance the linear flow of colours in the design.

Press-moulded, laminated bowl in which black slip has been used between the segments. By MAGGIE BARNES (UK), 1985. (Photo: Dr Paul Köster)

'Eroded Strata'. Bowl form in laminated stoneware clays (coloured with Mason stains and oxides) and sand-blasted after oxidized firing to cone 9. Diameter 61 cm (24 in). By VIRGINIA MITCHEM (UK), 1986. (Photo: Anthony Lauro)

Another method of using coloured clays in bowl forms is illustrated in the work of **Susan Nemeth** (UK). Her decorative pieces in porcelain are part abstract and part figurative, with ideas for design coming from a variety of sources, including derelict inner-city houses where layer upon layer of partially stripped wallpaper is often revealed with its many colours and torn edges. She has also been influenced by teaching mentally handicapped women, whose drawings she describes as being 'direct, unusual, beautiful and innocent, delicate and bold'. She has developed a lengthy process for the decoration of her bowl forms and this becomes an integral part of the whole piece. Layers of differently coloured slips are applied to each side of a rolled slab that is to be press-moulded later. Further colour is built up by rolling in shapes cut from thinner slabs of clay covered in many coloured slips, together with stained clay pieces. When the slab is rolled out again the slips and coloured clays stretch and become partly transparent, revealing other layers underneath. Surface slips can be sponged away after rolling, leaving some of the slip trapped around and outlining some of the inlays. Half tones are produced by rolling on textured cloth. Rubbing down with sandpaper between firings gives the surface of the piece a smooth matt finish and sometimes leads to further adjustments to the coloured layers.

Porcelain bowl, press-moulded and inlaid, with various coloured body stains. Fired to cone 8 (1250°C). Diameter 30 cm (11¾ in). By SUSAN NEMETH (UK), 1984. (Photo: Kenneth Grundy)

Porcelain bowl, press-moulded and inlaid, with coloured body stains. The flowers are black and green, the stripes blue and orange. Fired to cone 8 (1250°C). Diameter 35 cm (13¾ in). By SUSAN NEMETH (UK), 1984. (Photo: Anthony Phillips)

Left: Narrow-necked bottle, slip-cast porcelain with coloured inlays. The surface has been carved out and replaced by an inlaid design based on animals in a landscape. Fired in reduction to cone 9. Height 36 cm (14¼ in). By SONY MANNING (Australia), 1985.

Far left: Porcelain bottle vase, cast and inlaid with striped animal in a landscape of brown, blue, green and white on black. Fired in reduction to cone 6. Height 28 cm (11 in). By SONY MANNING (Australia), 1985.

Sony Manning (Australia) works rather differently with coloured inlays. Landscape has had a compelling influence on her ideas. It has become 'a form of autobiography' because many of her pieces are symbolic references to the high country where she spent much of her childhood. She depicts land formations, geological cross sections of ridges and rock strata, together with animals ('they were once in the form of horses or deer but now belong to no particular species. They have become more of a composite'). She prefers to explore the *idea* of vessels, with only casual reference to recognized function, while concentrating on basically cylindrical forms.

Colours are very important to Sony Manning and especially their effects in combination. To ensure greater definition and truer colours, she uses a fine, white-burning body with inlays. Care has to be taken when inlaying coloured clays because maturing temperatures may be affected and rates of expansion or contraction will often differ according to the proportions and natures of the metallic oxides used to stain the body. Tensions can be set up between different colours laid side by side and she finds it necessary to compensate for this by thickening the wall. Originally, she referred to an old, Egyptian glass-making technique, where glass rods are fused together and slices taken through these in cross section, and began adapting coloured clays likewise. Since then she has discovered other possibilities for constant and individual development of inlaid designs. Sometimes the emphasis is on line alone. She often includes abstracted animal shapes which are carved out and inlaid. Recent landscape imagery appears rather barren and lonely, with animals more remote.

Porcelain cup, inlaid with a design of animals in a landscape. The broader shapes of the landscape were carved out and inlaid first, then the other figurative elements were added. Fired in reduction to cone 9. Height 10 cm (4 in). By SONY MANNING (Australia), 1985.

Curved form, slab-built in high-fired red
clay with inlay, part glazed with
white-turquoise glaze, part in enamel
colours. By JACQUI PONCELET (UK), 1981.
(Photo: David Ward, courtesy of the Crafts
Council)

Below: Porcelain bowl with traditional
wood-fired lustres from smoke-reduced
pigments. Diameter 36 cm (14¼ in).
By SUTTON TAYLOR (UK), 1985.

Above: Square porcelain bowl, press-moulded from laminated, colour-stained clays initially rolled into a flat sheet. The unglazed surface has been smoothed and polished with a fine grade of wet-and-dry silicon carbide paper both after the bisque and the final firing to cone 8. In order to minimize warping during firing the piece is supported on a 'nest' of sand while in the kiln. 35.5 cm (14 in) square. By ANNE MERCER (**Australia**), 1986. (Photo: Grant Hancock)

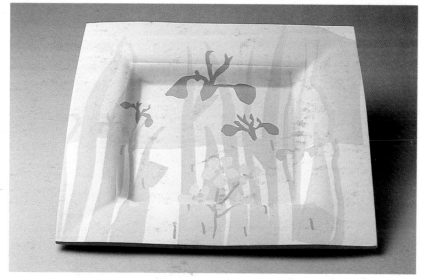

Slab-built porcelain plate with inlaid 'iris' design of coloured porcelain. 35.5 cm (14 in) square. By ANNE MERCER (**Australia**), 1983. (Photo: Grant Hancock)

Anne Mercer's (Australia) bowls begin as flat, rolled slabs of laminated, coloured porcelain in which the design is completed before being press-moulded into shape. Patterns are worked out intuitively, often in response to an amalgam of different experiences. Her garden (and her excellent collection of house plants of various shapes), her children, literature, or 'just messing about' with clay may all suggest ideas for her work. Her slabbed bowls have to be fired very carefully, set in supporting pockets of silica sand to minimize warping. Colours and patterns are sharply defined with no glaze to soften their impact. Instead, the pots are thoroughly polished with wet and dry Carborundum paper to give the surfaces a smooth sheen.

Textural variations

Another method which produces a visual effect similar to inlays is that used by **Gordon Cooke** (UK). In this case colours are brushed across one surface of a thick wad of plastic clay (usually porcelain), which is then inverted onto a smooth, plaster slab. This encourages the coloured side to dry quite quickly so that subsequent rolling out into a sheet causes the coloured areas to break into an interesting texture. Cooke has been able to develop this technique to the point where he can accurately control the nature and directional flow of the rolled textures.

Rolling out soft sheets of clay onto dry clay powder or fragments of dried clay produces rich textural variations. Finely extruded filaments of clay can be arranged into shapes and patterns and allowed to stiffen or even dry out completely before a soft, pre-rolled sheet of clay is placed over the top and gently rolled until the fragments adhere, impressed into the surface. They will be thinly outlined where contact between the particles and the softer clay is not total. These fine lines can be further emphasized by filling them with a wash of oxides or ceramic stains in either the raw or the bisque state and by clearing the top surface. Alternatively, coloured clays can be used for either the 'inlays' or the slab for a different kind of contrast.

Below left: Porcelain 'Persian' bottle. Height 24 cm (9½ in). By GORDON COOKE (UK), 1986.

Below: Porcelain 'Medusa' bottle. Height 24 cm (9½ in). By GORDON COOKE (UK), 1986.

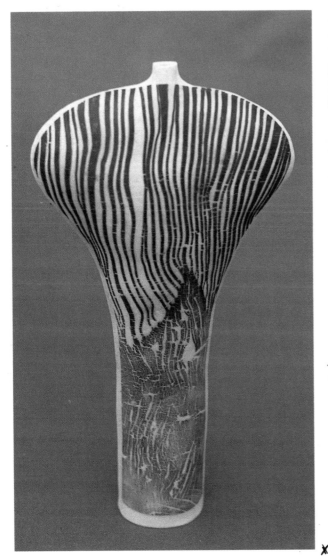

Slip-cast porcelain bottles with black-stained body and satin-matt black glaze reduction-fired to 1320°C. Strips of textile fabrics soaked in porcelain slip have been draped diagonally over the forms to relieve their severity and give textural interest. Height 35.5 cm (14 in). By PAULINE PELLETIER (Canada), 1986.

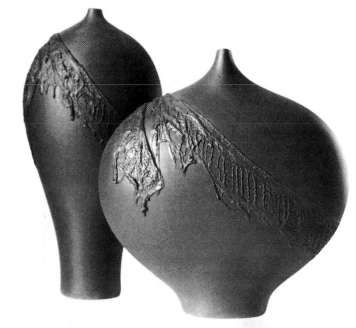

Bottle form, coil-built from a coarse clay body containing perlite for extra textural interest, and coloured with iron and manganese. After being scraped when dry, the pot was brushed over with a white engobe and fired to cone 6 in oxidation. The lighter area was given a second coating of white engobe and refired. The whole surface was then hand-ground to a smooth texture. Height 18.5 cm (7¼ in). By LARRY ELSNER (USA), 1985.
(Photo: Andrew M. Whitlock)

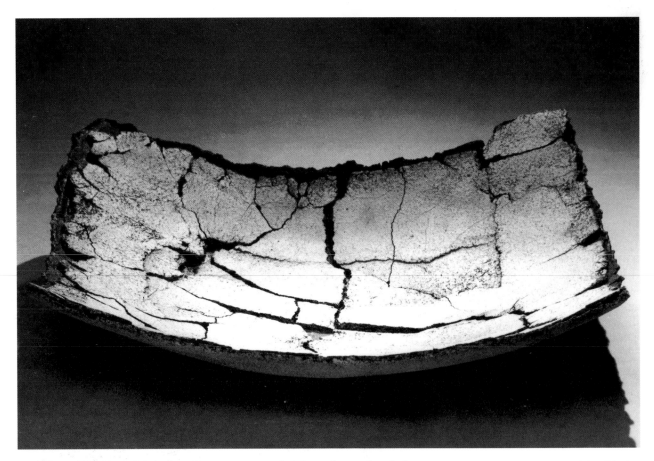

When rolling out a slab face down over a sprinkling of powdered clay, its surface quickly dries out as the powder absorbs moisture. Subsequently manipulating and shaping the slab causes the surface to fracture in a fascinating and characteristic way. This offers many opportunities for exploration and development of both form and surface. Granular or heavily grogged clay bodies which are allowed to stiffen slightly in the form of rolled slabs respond in a rather different fashion when manipulated, but the side or surface which is stretched the most will also fracture so that this feature can be utilized as an integral part of the design process.

Double-walled stoneware bowl, hand-built in coarse clays, with manganese oxide accentuating the linear elements. 45×43 cm (17¾×17 in). By YVETTE MINTZBERG (Canada), 1983.

Stoneware bowls, hand-built, with textured and modelled rims. Maximum diameter 36 cm (14¼ in). By LEN CASTLE (New Zealand), 1985.

There are a great many other textural treatments, both physical and visual, that can be used effectively to enliven ceramic surfaces. The whole may be covered with texture or selected areas only treated, to contrast with other parts left plain. One of the most simple methods I have often used myself on porcelain is the application of a crackle glaze. This can be stained with various pigments to accentuate the natural network of crazed lines that appears in the glaze. In general terms, the glaze is composed of materials which are calculated to shrink in firing to a greater degree than the body of the pot it covers. If that same glaze is applied too thinly the crackles may not develop. The size of the spaces between the crazed or broken lines can often be increased and controlled to a certain extent by a heavier application of glaze.

Porcelain bowl, wheel-thrown, with crackle glaze and unglazed bronze rim (painted with three parts manganese dioxide, one part copper carbonate with three parts china clay to thicken), fired to cone 9 in an electric kiln. This is followed by a lustre firing to 750°C to fix the gold banding. Diameter 23 cm (9 in). By PETER LANE (UK), 1985.

Wheel-thrown vessels with dry, barium glaze and copper carbonate splatter, fired in oxidation to cone 9. This dry glaze contains (by weight) fifty parts barium carbonate, fifty parts china clay, twenty parts potash feldspar and forty parts nepheline syenite, to which is added 4 per cent copper carbonate. Height of taller vessel 28 cm (11 in). By MARIANNE COLE (Australia), 1984. (Photo: Michael Kluvanek)

Normally, this glaze surface is reserved for the decorative treatment of stoneware or porcelain because the body of the pot beneath is fused to an impermeable state, but it also has its attractions for work in raku where functional aspects are less important. In the latter case, the crackles become stained black by carbon penetration during firing. It is more usual to stain higher-fired wares with inks or finely ground oxides mixed with oil or water. When oxides have been used to stain the crackled lines it is possible to refire the piece and apply a different colour to the fresh crackle lines that will appear on cooling. The first staining will soften or blur a little as the glaze melts, but the second will appear as a sharper, linear overlay. Of course, a similar effect can be achieved by using two different coloured inks: the first applied as soon as the pot is removed from the kiln (with a cloth to protect the glaze from sticky hands) and the second a day or two later when further crazing has developed.

A different kind of all-over texture can be seen in the convoluted pot made by **Joanna Constantinidis** (UK) from a wheel-thrown form then altered. A fine-toothed saw blade held against a revolving clay cylinder produces this sort of surface. The regularly spaced incised lines help to define the form and increase the visual interest.

Vessel form, wheel-thrown and altered.
By JOANNA CONSTANTINIDIS **(UK), 1976.**
(Photo: Crafts Council)

Stoneware basket vessel with sand-blasted tenmoku-type glaze, fired in reduction to cone 11. 46×35.5×30.5 cm (18×14× 12 in). By TIM MATHER (USA), 1985.

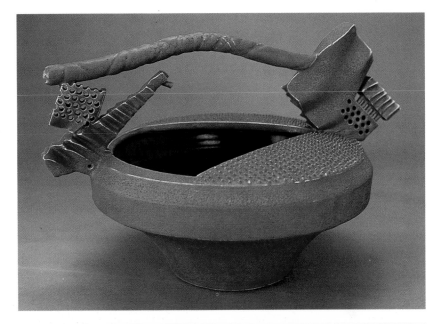

Below: Large, coil-built raku bowl. Interest is enhanced by the interplay of black and white and the different character of the crackled lines. Diameter 58 cm (23 in). By DAVID ROBERTS (UK), 1985.

Above: Stoneware bowl, wheel-thrown, with wax-resist pattern under the satin-matt glaze. Height 18.5 cm (7¼ in). By WERNER NOWKA (West Germany), 1985. (Photo: Gertrud Glasgow)

Above right: Porcelain bowl with matt black feldspathic glaze. The hard-edged severity of the form is complemented by the geometric counterchange in black and white contained within the vertical wall section, while the interior, foot and lower wall remain a solid black. Diameter 23 cm (9 in). By HILDEGARD EGGEMANN (West Germany), 1985.

Hand-built stoneware vessel with copper oxide under a matt white glaze. Fired in an electric kiln to 1250°C. Height 21 cm (8¼ in). By JOHN WARD (UK).

Ceramic stains and underglaze colours

There are some excellent-quality commercially prepared stains available now that offer a good range of reliable colours able to withstand high temperatures. I have found that the best of these, in the form of underglaze stains ready-mixed with painting medium, give predictable results when sprayed through an airbrush, or sponge-printed, or when brush-painted directly onto the surface of a clean, white porcelain bisque. I prefer to work on the bisque because a preliminary rubbing down with abrasive paper can be carried out prior to decorating with stains. Of course, it is essential to ensure that all traces of dust are removed before colour is applied.

The quality and versatility of any particular type of airbrush are important factors which will condition the kind of work possible. I use a variety of airbrushes from the cheapest, which produces a non-adjustable, fan-shaped spray, to the more elaborate models, which allow me to control minutely the thickness of line. The best of these can be adjusted in use by increasing the finger pressure with a trigger action. This is a very useful attribute in freehand drawing, but also works well when directing the airbrush over confined areas of masking where other colours have already been applied. I prefer to use water-based mixtures when airbrushing onto porcelain bisque because I find that oil-based colours take longer to dry. The latter are, however, better suited to spraying, especially in the form of enamels, onto tiles and other glazed wares.

Hard-edged designs are easily produced with the aid of paper masking tape of the kind used in the automobile trade. Tapes of many different widths are readily available and they can be cut into various shapes. There are also several types of reusable plastic tapes normally used for graphic design work, but, unless the bisque surface of the pot is totally free of dust particles, these will suffice for no more than two or three occasions and so hardly justify the extra expense. Different ready-made shapes in adhesive paper or in plastic materials can be bought in stationery stores and these can be very effective masks when used with discretion. The main disadvantage of these prepared shapes is that the material tends to be unable to withstand much overspraying without becoming loaded with wet colour that can run off and heavily stain the adjacent areas.

Ceramic stains which have been mixed with a good medium that does not permit the pigment to be easily dusted off when dry can be overlaid with further masking tapes and will accept further colours airbrushed on top. This can produce interesting colour combinations and have an effect rather like screen-printing, where colours alter in the overlapped areas and layered effects with an illusion of considerable depth can be achieved. One of the main difficulties, likely to be encountered as the masking becomes more complex, is in trying to remember enough of the hidden design and the juxtaposition of the colours previously applied. I rarely draw a pattern on paper prior to working on a piece because I prefer to approach the work as if it were a painting in any other medium, manipulating shapes, colours and tonal contrasts in an intuitive way to suit the form and to try to resolve the idea I have in mind.

Direct brush painting with ceramic stains and oxides offers other alternatives to the effects and kind of surface that can be produced by an airbrush, but with this technique it is more difficult to disguise any uneven applications of colour. However, such variations in the brushwork may in some instances be more appropriate and they can convey a more lively feeling to the work.

'Confetti'. Porcelain bowl with airbrushed design in orange and blue ceramic stains, fired to cone 7 in an electric kiln. Unglazed but polished with wet-and-dry silicon carbide paper. Diameter 18.5 cm (7¼ in). By PETER LANE (UK), 1986.

Dorothy Hafner (USA) is 'very concerned with function, both physical and "metaphysical"'. She likes 'objects with high performance capability. You can use them with ease and they bring real dynamism to the table with or without use; sort of like a sports car – more than just transportation'. Her unusual porcelain bowls are constructed from carefully shaped individual slabs onto which is painted a vibrant patchwork of patterns. Both form and pattern are intentionally 'off-beat'. Her brilliantly clear decoration, with multiple elements juxtaposed in bold arrangements, is partly influenced by Primitive Art, highly ornamental seventeenth- and eighteenth-century European porcelains, and 1950s aerodynamic design. These elements often bring to mind patterns found in certain printed textiles. She likes her pots to have 'a highly charged surface which employs both colour and pattern'.

The forms are initially worked out and a mock-up is made with shapes cut out from tar paper, one for each side. These tar paper units are then used as templates for cutting the slabs of clay: the slabs are rolled onto the paper so that they adhere and the waste is cut away from the edges with a fettling knife. The paper acts as a support for each slab during the fabrication process and allows Dorothy Hafner to manipulate it without distortion caused by stretching or finger marks. By this method, softer slabs can be handled and joined together with assurance and ease. Concave and convex plaster formers are also used to support the clay during construction and drying. When the piece is assembled and the slabs have stiffened sufficiently, the tar paper is simply peeled away from the outside and the piece left to dry slowly under polythene sheeting. A plaster press-mould is used to support the bottom slab and form a curved base, which is allowed to overhang the mould a little so that it can be removed easily once it stiffens. Clay units (later to be discarded) are used during firing to support the curved sections of the form.

All these pieces are hand painted with underglaze colours onto a low-temperature bisque before being sprayed with a clear glaze and fired to the high temperature necessary for maturation of the porcelain.

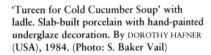

'Tureen for Cold Cucumber Soup' with ladle. Slab-built porcelain with hand-painted underglaze decoration. By DOROTHY HAFNER (USA), 1984. (Photo: S. Baker Vail)

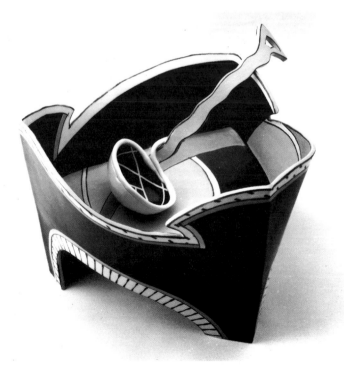

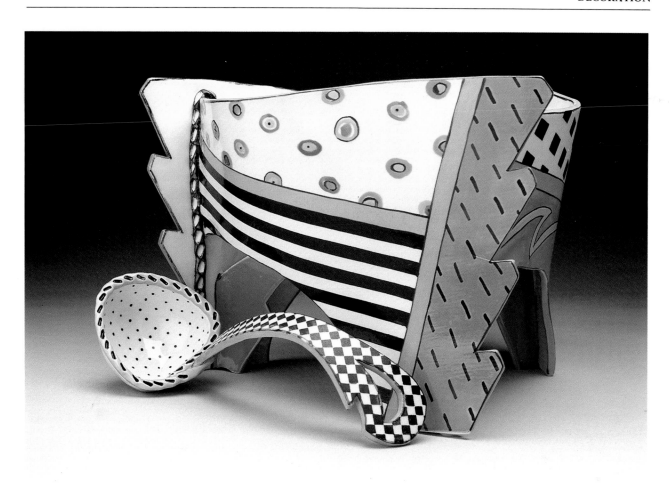

Although she finds porcelain 'very limiting' compared with earthenware or stoneware clays, she continues to use it, despite the difficulties, for its strength in the final, fired state.

'Lightning Bolt Punch Bowl with Spoon'. Hand-built porcelain vessel with underglaze decoration. The form has been divided into sections with contrasting patterns and colours which accentuate its unusual shape and construction. By DOROTHY HAFNER (USA), 1984. (Photo: S. Baker Vail)

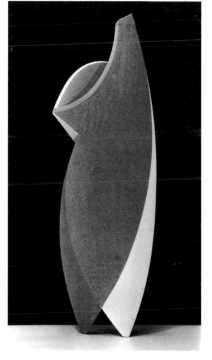

Far left: Vessel in grogged red earthenware clay, slab- and coil-built and beaten to modify curves. Coloured with turquoise-green slip. Height 40 cm (15¾ in). By PHILIPPA CRONIN (UK), 1984.

Left: Vessel in grogged red earthenware clay, slab- and coil-built and beaten to modify curves. Coloured with pink and grey slips. Height 68 cm (26¾ in). By PHILIPPA CRONIN (UK), 1985.

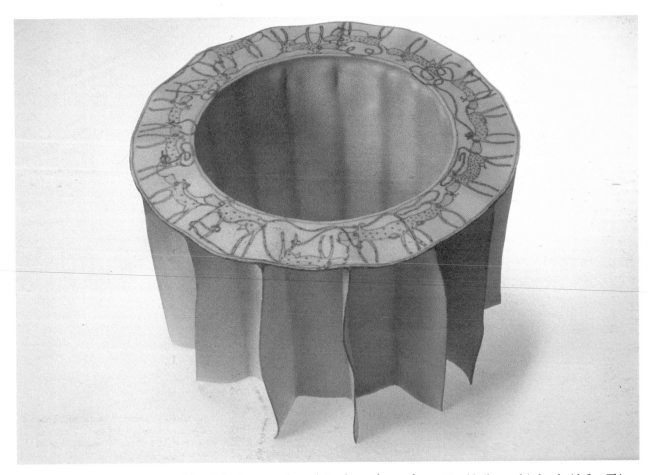

The increasing abundance of brightly decorated, multi-coloured vessels has been a noticeable aspect of other, recent studio ceramics, with many of the pieces having patterned sections of great complexity. This style of decoration, where apparently random areas of unconnected patterns vie for attention, has become extremely popular during the past decade. This is due in part to an inevitable reaction against the browns, blacks and speckled oatmeal glazes common to so much stoneware produced throughout the world over the past thirty years or so. Interest has been further fuelled by the increased availability of reliable, high-quality ceramic stains prepared and energetically marketed by the ceramics industry. Certainly, direct painting with oxides, underglaze colours and body stains is much more common at the time of writing. Similarly, glazes which are dipped, poured, sprayed, painted or sponge-printed one on top of another are frequently used with considerable exuberance, although with slightly less predictable results. The development of a good range of white-firing bodies, especially porcelains, has also provided studio potters with the essential background for displaying colour whose clarity would otherwise be sullied by the excess quantities of iron which are present in most natural clays.

However, unless these complicated designs are applied with a fair degree of sensitivity and in sympathy with the vessel, the form can be submerged and lost under a desperate kind of visual cacophony. Too often we see a fresh style emerge and gain strength through the efforts, intuition and beliefs of its innovator only to be seized upon by others who, less competent and without understanding, produce what amounts to little more than a shallow pastiche of the original.

Hand-built porcelain bowl with fins. This piece is made from extremely thin sheets of clay and is very translucent. The broad, flat rim has whimsical drawings of animals forming a pattern of lines and shapes. Fired to cone 9 in oxidation. Diameter 15 cm (6 in). By BELINDA MASON (Australia), 1984.

Slips and engobes

Slips or engobes are useful for providing smooth, dense and reliable areas of colour. They can be applied by brush, spray or by dipping. This is normally done at the leather-hard stage so that the body and engobe shrink at a more or less equal rate while drying. On bone-dry or bisqued pots the plastic clay content of the slip must be reduced and replaced by feldspar and calcined clays in addition to other materials to prevent excessive shrinkage that would cause it to flake away from the body beneath.

Left: **Porcelain bottle vase with brushed slip decoration in relief under a celadon glaze. Height 23 cm (9 in). By** HARLAN HOUSE **(Canada), 1986.**

Far left: **Tall porcelain bottle with brushed slip decoration in relief under a celadon glaze. Height 46 cm (18 in). By** HARLAN HOUSE **(Canada), 1986.**

Painting with slips made from differently coloured, naturally occurring clays in earth tones is one of the oldest methods used by potters from various cultures to decorate their wares. Some of the finest unglazed vessels decorated with slips in creams, reds, browns, siennas, ochres, oranges and black can be found among the work of pre-Columbian potters of the Americas. Making and firing processes seem 'primitive', but they contribute qualities that would be difficult to duplicate any other way.

Shallow bowl, wheel-thrown, carved and pierced, with textured copper slip decoration. Once-fired (unglazed) to 1260°C in reduction. Diameter 20 cm (8 in). By MAGGIE BARNES **(UK), 1986.**

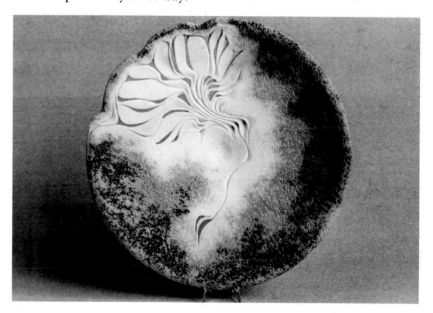

Two parabolic bottles with mocha diffusion decoration. The porcelain forms were thrown in two parts (the base being made upside down) and the upper part was flattened into an oval section. These forms were developed from an interplay of geometry and classical proportion, with reversing curves making a subtle allusion to the human figure. Heights 46 cm (18 in) and 38 cm (15 in). By ROBIN HOPPER (Canada).

Below: Hand-built stoneware bowls with painted slip decoration. By ELIZABETH FRITSCH (UK). (Photo: Crafts Council)

Diogenes Farri (Australia) was born in Valparaíso, Chile, but emigrated to Australia in 1971 where he is now teaching. His own creative work in ceramics involves the use of coloured slips in a way which reaches back to his own cultural background. He sees this as an opportunity to preserve the technique itself while enjoying the pictorial possibilities offered to present it in a contemporary context. He is attracted to round, egg-shaped forms and these have always been the starting point for his work. If he makes a non-utilitarian piece which happens to present the image of a bottle, that is not necessarily the product of any conscious effort or need to categorize the object as such.

The introduction of new material processes and themes in his work is evidence of his attempt to extend the original technique and to rediscover some of those unique qualities achieved by pre-Columbian potters in the Andes region of South America. Utilizing basic materials and simple technology, these potters were able to produce the most astonishing forms and images full of power, dynamism and vitality. Their 'craft' objects transcend the limits of dexterity and skill to become works of art, standing as equals with other forms of visual expression, reflecting as they do a remarkable sense of faith and conviction. Inspired by the work of these earlier craftsmen, Diogenes Farri applies coloured slips at the leather-hard stage and compresses them into the body by burnishing with a smoothly rounded pebble. Sometimes, an initial coating of slip provides a background colour onto which other colours are overlaid. Burnishing is carried out several times as the pot dries because the sheen so obtained will otherwise be lost due to the moisture evaporating. Reburnishing until the piece is almost dry consolidates the sheen and helps seal the surface. Commercial lustres and enamels are added later for second and third firings.

Above: **Hand-built bottle form, painted with coloured slips and thoroughly burnished several times with a smooth pebble until almost dry. Height 48 cm (19 in). By** DIOGENES FARRI **(Australia). (Photo: Edith Farri)**

Above left: **Hand-built bottle form, constructed from a mixture of terracotta and stoneware clays, decorated with coloured slips which are burnished with a smooth pebble several times until almost dry (in order to retain the sheen produced by this method), with commercial gold lustre pigments. Height 48 cm (19 in). By** DIOGENES FARRI **(Australia), 1985. (Photo: Edith Farri)**

The work of **Siddig El'nigoumi** (UK) has been well documented in my book *Studio Ceramics* (Collins, 1983) and elsewhere, but his techniques and approaches to decoration are worth examining again here. He makes a variety of vessel forms and is, perhaps, best known for his press-moulded dishes and bowls.

The piece illustrated opposite is a double-necked bottle which has been decorated with a sgraffito pattern through slip. This is a traditional kind of bottle, or 'ibreeq' as it is called, used in the Sudan to store water economically. (Although both the Blue Nile and White Nile flow through the Sudan it is a region of Africa which suffers extreme water shortages.) The bottle has one large hole for filling and a smaller one for pouring. For El'nigoumi this is not only a useful utensil but also a beautiful form to decorate. The hand-built, earthenware body of the vessel has been covered with a fine red slip (made from fine-textured Fremington clay, which has a low firing temperature), stained a brighter colour than the underlying form – the natural colour of the slip was intensified with an addition of red iron oxide. When this had dried to a leather-hard condition it was thoroughly burnished with a pebble until the slip was well compacted to a shine with a silky, smooth surface. Drawing was done when the pot was dry by scratching through the slip to reveal the lighter colour of the body beneath.

This is a typical example of work by El'nigoumi, whose applied designs are always well organized with a sequence of evenly drawn linear patterns. Much of the inspiration for his patterned work comes from the decorated houses of Nubia in the Sudan where he spent his early life. The flooding of the Aswan Dam in the mid-1960s destroyed most of the beautifully decorated mud houses in that area so he feels it is important that he should attempt to record and reflect some of those patterns through his pots. He also acknowledges the influence that the calabash gourd has had on the forms and decoration of pots made in many parts of Africa and, ultimately, on his own work.

Burnishing and decorating by scratching through the smooth surface, El'nigoumi discovered that it is essential to relate the sensitivity and delicacy of the designs with the thickness of the pot. When using a number of differently coloured slips for burnishing, they should always be of exactly the same consistency or there is a risk that colours will be smudged together by uneven drying of adjacent areas. He has developed a method of carbonizing the surface of some of his pots with burning newsprint. The paper used for this should contain a high percentage of resin, because the resin vapours also help to seal the surface and enhance the shine.

Press-moulded dish, with a patterned and burnished design of elephants incised through slips. By SIDDIG EL'NIGOUMI (UK).

Stoneware bottle form: a burnished,
Sudanese 'ibreeq' jug, a traditional shape
employed to dispense the water as
economically as possible. Height 23 cm
(9 in). By SIDDIG EL'NIGOUMI (UK).

Calabash-shaped stoneware vessel,
decorated by burnishing and scratching
through slips. Height 23 cm (9 in).
By SIDDIG EL'NIGOUMI (UK).
(Photo: Andrew Dowsett)

Interior of porcelain bowl, sprayed with terra sigillata, and with brushwork in bronze pigment (fifty-fifty copper and manganese oxides) fired to cone 10 in an electric kiln and then trail-glazed with chrome red and fired to cone 010. The residual fuming comes from the chrome in conjunction with the tin-opacified sigillata. Diameter 38 cm (15 in). By ROBIN HOPPER (Canada), 1986.

Painting with lustres and glazes

Freehand brushwork requires confident handling and a sure touch if it is not to appear clumsy and inarticulate. Calligraphic marks made with fluent movements of the arm are generally better than tighter ones made with the fingers alone. **Derek Clarkson** (UK) prefers a smooth surface for the brush decoration which has always been a feature of his work, presenting him with a never-ending challenge, variety and a rewarding form of expression. He particularly enjoys painting on unfired glaze. This has a certain 'bite', requiring a light, spontaneous touch and intuitive judgement of surface curvature, brush pressure and the composition of successive strokes, as well as awareness of the shapes of the spaces in between. He likes to use shiny tenmoku and copper red glazes that are highlighted by reflections which are animated as the observer moves. Patterns composed of repeated units, lent further interest by perspective distortion on a rounded form, are often used.

Bowl made in red earthenware. The piece is tin-glazed and wood-fired, the design brushed on with gold lustre flashing pink behind the brush marks. By ALAN CAIGER-SMITH (UK), 1978. (Photo: City Museum, Stoke-on-Trent)

Stoneware bottle with wood-ash glaze, cobalt and iron brush decoration, and kaki glaze spots. Fired in reduction to cone 10 (1300°C). Height 27 cm (10½ in). By DEREK CLARKSON (UK), 1985. (Photo: John Coles)

Below: Porcelain bowl with celadon glaze, decorated with cobalt and iron brushwork and kaki glaze spots. Fired in reduction to cone 10 (1300°C). By DEREK CLARKSON (UK), 1985.

Metallic lustres of one kind or another satisfy the decorative needs of many potters, but it is not so easy to achieve a happy marriage with the underlying form, especially when commercial preparations are used. Often these lustres, painted on top of the fired glaze prior to refiring at 750°C, appear to be quite separate, sitting on the surface. A livelier feeling of integration can be achieved by working away at the unfired lustre and breaking its surface tension with solvents. Fresh colours can be touched in to give delicate variations of colour and tone. This is a successful technique developed by **Geoffrey Swindell** (UK) and which I fully describe in *Studio Porcelain* (Pitman, 1980). It is well suited to relatively small pots, but is more difficult to control over larger areas.

Mary Rich (UK), too, likes to use gold and many other lustres over coloured glazes, especially when she can exploit the subtle relationship of lustres and glazes that are both dark in tone. Richly glowing patterns composed of repeated units, often geometric, band her bottle and bowl forms. The intricate, crisply defined brushwork complements the simple clarity of profile and is reminiscent of some examples of Islamic decoration. The bottle illustrated here has been divided into a number of horizontally banded areas with bright, gold lustre painted over a dark glaze. The broadest band of solid gold lustre encircles the pot and gives some visual weight to the lower part just above the base at the point where, in some other bottle forms, an inward turn towards the foot might be expected. This band also supports the delicately painted tracery, forming a looped pattern of thin gold lines above, which is divided into three sections by narrower bands of gold. This stops naturally at the shoulder where the profile makes a sharp change of direction.

I have found that most commercial lustre colours can be overfired to a temperature of around 1000°C to obtain a range of different tonal pinks. The colours also lose their reflective brilliance at this temperature and become an attractive satin matt when the base glaze is not excessively glossy.

Opposite: Porcelain bottle, wheel-thrown, with a barium carbonate glaze over slip containing copper and manganese fired in reduction atmosphere to cone 10 in a propane gas kiln. On-glaze lustres of gold and copper were brushed on for the finely controlled decoration reminiscent of certain Islamic patterns. Height 43 cm (17 in). By MARY RICH (UK), 1985. (Photo: Matthew Donaldson)

Porcelain bowl brushed with cobalt/manganese slip under a barium carbonate glaze fired in reduction to cone 10. Painted with gold and copper lustres in a geometric pattern and refired to 750°C. Having observed working methods employed for porcelain in China, Mary Rich now turns (trims) her pots far more than she used to, including the insides of her bowls. She sees vessel forms as 'entirely abstract objects'. Firings are conducted very quickly in a ceramic fibre kiln: bisque in three hours and reduction glost to cone 10 in four hours. Diameter 23 cm (9 in). By MARY RICH (UK), 1985.

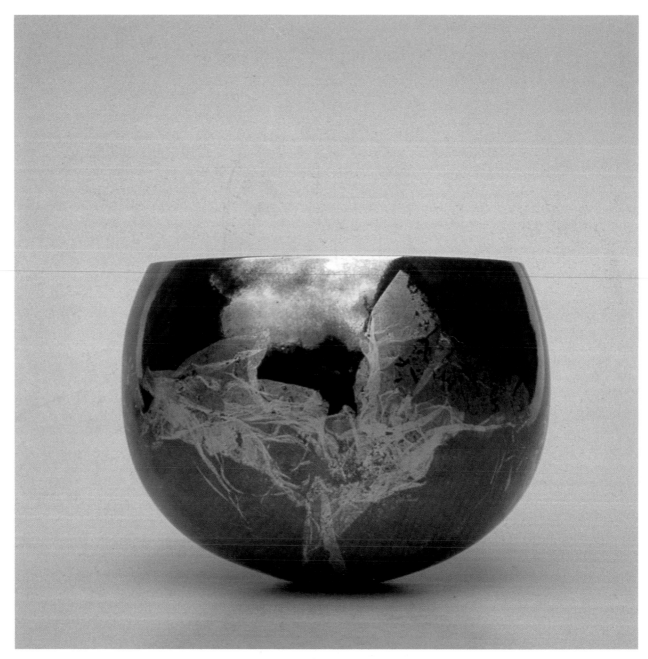

Porcelain bowl with lustred glaze and applied 23-carat gold-leaf decoration (fired on to the glaze at 700°C). Height 10 cm (4 in). By GREG DALY (**Australia**), 1985.

Greg Daly (Australia) makes lustre-glazed pots which are fired up to 1060°C and allowed to cool to around 750°C, at which point a heavy reduction atmosphere is introduced and held until the temperature drops to 600°C. Some of these glazes contain silver, bismuth, and copper in an alkaline base, while others just have copper or combinations of materials including cobalt and manganese nitrates. He prepares his other lustres by melting pine resin with added amounts of bismuth nitrate and zinc acetate. This mixture is left for thirty to sixty minutes until it becomes a shiny dark brown, then lavender oil is slowly added. The proportions are approximately 10 g of resin to 30 ml of lavender oil. This is painted or sprayed onto the glazed porcelain pot and 23-carat gold leaf (as normally used by sign writers and purchased from paint suppliers) is applied to the surface and fired to 700°C. The resin lustre helps to fuse the gold leaf to the pot, so that it appears to have considerable depth within the glaze.

Porcelain bowls with lustred glaze and applied 23-carat gold-leaf decoration (fired on to the glaze at 700°C). Height 10 cm (4 in). By GREG DALY (**Australia**), 1985.

Porcelain bowl with cobalt dark blue matt glaze and gold lustre. The character of this simple, cylindrical vessel has been altered by the addition of two vestigial lugs. Diameter 18 cm (7 in). By LES BLAKEBROUGH (**Australia**), 1986.

Traditional wood-fired, smoke-reduced lustre pigments are found to be more satisfactory by potters wishing to encourage the fire to make a greater contribution to glaze quality. It is impossible to predict results completely, but they can be magnificent. It is a technique imaginatively used by **Sutton Taylor** (UK), who manages to control a wide range of colours and visual textures while working almost exclusively on bowl forms which he conceives to take the role of paintings or sculpture. These conventional vessel forms contain complex images which seem to change as the viewer's position alters. He uses a rather 'short', friable, earthenware marl, which can be worked on the wheel for only a comparatively short time and demands to be thrown with very little water. Its failings in this direction are compensated by particular qualities that assist the development of lustres. Taylor does not consider his painting of a bowl to be 'decoration', but rather as the purpose for its being. Without diminishing the importance of the form itself he uses it as a vehicle for his painting, as a kind of three-dimensional canvas. All his pots are glaze-fired to 1150°C, with the wood-fired lustre reduction taking place at 735°C.

Moulded porcelain bowl with white matt glaze over brushed oxide design. Fired in reduction to 1330°C. 43×10 cm (17×4 in). By DEREK DAVIS (UK), 1985. (Photo: Hugo Barclay)

A similar attitude prevails among those potters who 'paint' with resisted and overlaid glazes. This kind of work requires fine control over the placement, flow and interaction of glazes, so a flatter surface is usually preferred. Large platters or wide, low-walled bowls allow unhindered access to expansive areas, inviting both abstract and figurative forms of expression. Most are intended to be displayed upright in a stand or hung on a wall like a picture so that the textures, patterns, shapes and nuances of colour can best be seen. Thrown pieces often have a flared, encircling rim which acts as a frame.

Porcelain bowl with traditional wood-fired
lustres from smoke-reduced pigments.
By SUTTON TAYLOR (UK), 1985.

Below: Porcelain bowl with traditional
wood-fired lustres from smoke-reduced
pigments. Diameter 33 cm (13 in).
By SUTTON TAYLOR (UK), 1985.

Bryan Trueman (Australia) is well known for his interpretation of the Australian landscape on both porcelain and stoneware. He uses wax-resist techniques with a complex glazing process involving a number of overlaid glazes having different flow characteristics. Waxed areas appear hard-edged before firing, but these are softened as the glaze melts. His figurative images are acquired 'by an osmosis-like principle. One is not fully aware of the intense response to a visual situation which might lie dormant for quite some time until, for some unknown reason, it explodes its presence into one's work.'

Large, shallow stoneware bowl, with multiple overlaid glazes producing rich colours and textural interest. Diameter 50 cm (19¾ in). By BRYAN TRUEMAN (Australia), 1984.

Shallow porcelain bowl, with landscape design, produced by pouring, painting and wax resisting, with multiple glazes and thicknesses. Diameter 38 cm (15 in). By BRYAN TRUEMAN (**Australia**), 1985.

'Metchosin Mists'. Slab-built porcelain bottle with a thrown neck, with multiple glazes, poured, trailed, brushed, dipped, spattered, wax-resisted with glaze intaglio. Eight thin glazes were applied and fired at the same time. This example is one of a series developed from geometric and classical proportions with an allusion to cloaked human figures. The flattened form was specifically designed to display two-dimensional imagery. Height 46 cm (18 in). By ROBIN HOPPER (Canada).

Robin Hopper (Canada) also uses landscape as the basis for glaze painting that is evocative of the mountainous regions of western Canada. Large platters and flat-sided, slab-built bottles provide him with ideal surfaces for such pictorial work because the periphery of these pieces acts as a natural boundary to contain freely painted matter.

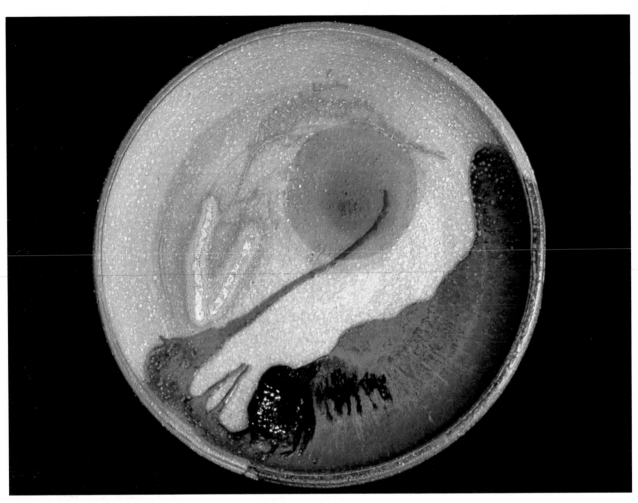

Stoneware platter, with poured glazes
suggesting elements of landscape, gas- and
wood-fired. Diameter 64 cm (25¼ in).
By MILTON MOON (**Australia**).

Milton Moon is another Australian potter whose work reflects what he describes as 'the awesome harshness of the dry inland landscape of Australia' close to his home. His work often includes sensitive brushwork patterns derived from plants.

Footed bowl, hand-built from slabs and
coils of white stoneware clay, with brushed
and trailed coloured slips, wood-fired, and
with translucent glaze and exposed areas of
clay flashed orange by wood ash. Fired in
reduction to cone 9. 30 cm (11¾ in) square.
By MERILYN WISEMAN (**New Zealand**), 1986.
(Photo: Howard Williams)

Stoneware bottle with net pattern in celadon glaze, wheel-thrown, fired to 1360°C in a reduction atmosphere. Height 28 cm (11 in). By GOTLIND WEIGEL (West Germany), 1985. (Photo: R. Zwillsperger)

Stoneware bowl with net decoration, glazed brown/blue and fired to 1360°C in a reduction atmosphere. Height 10 cm (4 in). By GOTLIND WEIGEL (West Germany), 1985. (Photo: R. Zwillsperger)

Applying one glaze on top of another, especially when one is a dry matt and the other of a glossy nature, usually produces much more visual interest than if the two were mixed together beforehand. This technique is particularly effective when used in conjunction with wax resists. Where the design requires positive changes of colour or surface, or where it is intended that brightly coloured, glossy glazes should remain clearly defined and not flow into each other, then a barrier of some sort must be used between them. It is possible to use painted lines of wax resist to preserve strips of unglazed body between the glazes, but this is often a lengthy and not totally reliable process when runny glazes are used. Piped or trailed lines of slip provide a stronger physical barrier. Both these methods can be used for vertical forms so long as the glazes do not run unduly. Some of the brightest colour combinations in shiny earthenware glazes separated by tube lining have been used on tiles which can be fired flat, reducing the problem of glaze runs.

One or more glazes can also be sprayed over other forms of resist, such as open-meshed fabrics and nets. Reasonably close contact between the resist material and the surface of the pot is essential, however, if the design is required to be sharp.

Coil-built bottle, low-fired in a mixture of
dung, leaves and wood chips for
twenty-four hours after burnishing. Height
27 cm (10½ in). By ROBYN STEWART (New
Zealand), 1985. (Photo: Howard Williams)

Firing and post-firing techniques

There is no doubt that methods of construction and techniques of
decoration can, in themselves, provide the motivation and ideas for a
number of potters. At the same time, their work will be conditioned to
some degree by the processes they employ. It is often the physical
requirements and the very limitations of those processes (and the need to
overcome problems as they arise) that can stimulate an imaginative
response. New technologies have also revolutionized several aspects of
pottery making for the studio potter.

Simple bowl form designed to hold plant
material without which the piece would be
incomplete. By GEERT ROYGENS (Belgium),
1985.

Above: Globular pot, wheel-thrown in a heavily grogged clay with the surface smoothed with rubber ribs. Colours were obtained in a pit-firing process with additions of simple chemicals (salt, soda ash, copper) and by controlling the length of firing. Maximum width 20 cm (8 in). By DAVID KURAOKA (USA), 1981. (Photo: Dean Oshiro)

Wheel-thrown stoneware platter, with hardwood-ash glaze and oxides, once-fired to cone 10 in a reduction atmosphere. The rich and regular pattern of runnels is typical of many wood-ash glazes. Diameter 51 cm (20 in). By SPRING STREET STUDIO (USA), 1986.

'Kashani Metamorphosis II'. Wheel-thrown bottle form with residual handles and spouts, and sgraffito decoration through multiple slips. Height 70 cm (27½ in). By ALAN PEASCOD (Australia), 1986.

Raku bowl, wheel-thrown. Various oxides were applied after the bisque firing before refiring to 1050°C in a gas kiln, and subsequent reduction in wood shavings to produce the colour variations. Diameter 9.5 cm (3¾ in). By ROBERT ALLAN (Australia), 1982. (Photo: Henry Jolles)

The improved insulation properties of ceramic fibre, now widely used in kilns, has encouraged radical alterations to traditional firing programmes. This fibre, usually in blanket or in slab form, is quite fragile and, although it can be safely used over long periods without serious damage to its surface being caused, it is often protected behind a layer of insulating brick. Pots can be fired much more rapidly in ceramic fibre kilns without risk or any noticeable loss of quality. **Alan Peascod** (Australia) has used fast firing methods for more than fifteen years and now his kiln cycle averages between one and a quarter and two and three quarter hours to 1250°C. He adopted this approach when he realized that accepted notions regarding glaze development in the heating process were largely irrelevant as far as his own work was concerned. He prefers to have the capability of firing any piece to glaze temperature at least twice a day in the same kiln, because he fires the work in series and each fired result subsequently dictates the needs of the next. He has also discovered that better glaze quality has resulted in those firings conducted when the kiln was still hot from the preceding one.

Most of Peascod's decorative processes revolve around the practice of manipulating the acid or alkaline content of the slip or glaze fluids. This is in order to control the flow characteristics of the fluid, which, in turn, dictate the final surface qualities. In much of his work he relies on post-firing techniques such as corrosion by chemical or mechanical means. Steel wool, wire brushes and silicon carbide gritstones are used in conjunction with engraving techniques to abrade glaze surfaces. Other methods include the application of hydrofluoric, nitric and sulphuric acids, together with resists. This uninhibited approach produces finished pieces which display richly textured areas of immense variety in colour and tone. The 'decoration' thus becomes an essential part of the whole form.

Salt-glazing has gained enormous popularity during the past twenty years or so due to the fresh approaches of potters in several countries. The most attractive effects are obtained with relief decoration where the nature of salt glaze is able to give it greater emphasis. **Suzy Atkins** (France) uses this method of glazing for her distinctive stoppered bottles or decanters. It is a fascinating exercise to explore the reactions of different materials at various temperatures and kiln atmospheres. The most familiar materials are wood ashes and salt, but many other substances of vegetable, animal or mineral origin are worthy of experimentation. An example of some of the beautiful surface qualities obtainable by the imaginative use of salt, wood ash and organic material is shown in the shallow bowl by **Tom Coleman** (USA).

Unusual materials not normally associated with ceramics also offer some interesting possibilities for any adventurous enough to experiment. Organic matter of various kinds such as seaweed, wood, or other plant material will contribute colour and texture in different ways according to its use. Placing a pot in a sealed saggar with organic matter like seeds or sawdust and traces of common salt or copper carbonate will cause the surface of the pot to be impregnated with a fairly random pattern of fumed colour when fired. A greater degree of control can be obtained by surrounding the pot with alternating layers of different materials. Sand and pieces of clay can be used to protect parts of the pot's surface from the action of the salts or combustible elements within the saggar. Some wonderful, if unpredictable, colour effects are possible, and the palette can be broadened further by judicious use of metallic oxides. This form of surface treatment, at its best, can completely clothe a pot in the most natural and complementary way.

Pair of decanters, thrown and incised (La Borne clay), with colours obtained from overlaid slips. The decoration includes wax-resist, paper-resist, etching, pouring and slip-trailing techniques. Salt-glaze-fired to 1320°C in a gas kiln and 'crash-cooled' to 1000°C at the end of the firing. Height of taller piece 34.5 cm (13⅝ in). By SUZY ATKINS (France), 1986. (Photo: Pierre Soissons)

Porcelain platter with salt and wood ash sprayed over black slip and with further organic matter on top, fired in reduction to cone 10 (1300°C). By TOM COLEMAN (USA), 1985. (Photo: Rick Paulson)

Most potters will have experienced raku firing at some time or another, but, to a growing number, raku (which is very process-orientated) has become the main vehicle for personal expression. **David Roberts** (UK) works with a coarse, open-textured clay body which lends itself to hand building large, simple forms able to withstand the considerable thermal shock of rapid firing and cooling. He enjoys working within the limitations that practical considerations place upon him and the range of forms which he has developed, because he finds that the discipline involved is actually a liberating influence. Even the decoration is derived directly from or related to the raku process itself. It provides him with a variety of colours and surfaces which he feels are sympathetic to his pots. His firing methods are adapted from Western raku techniques using large, 'top hat' kilns lined with ceramic fibre and designed for convenience and easy access. A dense post-firing reduction is carried out in purpose-built, sealed containers. The combination of white glaze with heavily stained crackling and blackened, raw areas is an attractive feature on some of his bowls.

I have met several potters who fire their work many times to achieve the surface qualities they desire. The most obvious of these multi-firing processes is to fire to stoneware or porcelain temperatures and then to fire progressively downwards with different materials that will fuse and contribute further to the piece at lower temperatures, until the final application may be enamel colours or lustres fired at 750°C. Ceramic surfaces having considerable visual depth can be created in this way.

Large, coil-built raku bowl with resist decoration and white crackled glaze. The sharply defined pattern, with white glaze and smoke-blackened, diagonal stripes, is arranged in a band round the still centre. Diameter 58 cm (23 in). By DAVID ROBERTS (UK), 1985.

Porcelain bottle, thrown, with smoked terra sigillata surface. Height 15 cm (6 in). By JEAN PAUL AZAIS (France), 1986. (Photo: Paul Palau)

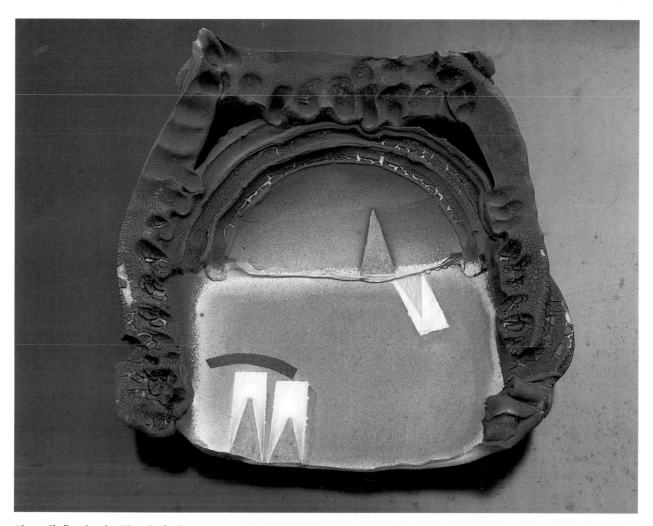

Above: Shallow bowl, with multi-fired slips, glazes and enamels. Approximately 51×41 cm (20×16 in). By BRIAN GARTSIDE (New Zealand), 1985.

Smoked porcelain bowl with layered lip and metallic thread. 'This piece was wheel-thrown and coils were added to form the rim. Grooves were incised in the lower wall and a mixture of terra sigillata and commercial stain was sprayed on. After bisque firing, it was packed tightly in a metal trash can with sawdust, which was ignited and allowed to smoulder for about three days. The pot was then washed and the metallic thread fixed into the grooves.' Diameter 14 cm (5½ in). By GAIL RUSSELL (USA), 1985.

'Funnel Vessel'. Slip-cast stoneware with a high-shrinkage, dry glaze, a black satin magnesia glaze, and airbrushed ceramic stains. Fired in reduction to cone 9. Height 19.5 cm (7¾ in). By GARRY BISH (Australia), 1985. (Photo: R. Aulsebrook)

Opposite above: Vessel in stoneware, hand-built, with bronze and black colour. Diameter 38 cm (15 in). By JENIFER JONES (UK). (Photo: L. Gresswell)

Below: 'Flache Taschenform'. Stoneware bowl with incised pattern under a celadon glaze fired in reduction to 1360°C. Height 15 cm (6 in). By GOTLIND WEIGEL (West Germany), 1985. (Photo: Jochen Schade)

Trumpet-necked bottle with oil-spot glaze fired to cone 10. Height 20 cm (8 in). By HORST KERSTAN (West Germany).

It can be seen that the 'vocabulary' of pottery form and decoration, with its materials, processes and techniques, can be translated in an infinite number of ways for truly personal expression. No matter how much has gone before or how long and established the traditions may be, individuals can still develop their own 'language' to communicate their particular feelings through the medium of ceramics. This language lives on and, occasionally, radical approaches revive or adapt ancient techniques, giving them a contemporary flavour. But, behind all this fascination for the materials and methods lie the beliefs and dedication of the potters seeking to extend their own perception of the world around them. They will respond subject to their personalities and conditioned by those influences that impinge most closely upon their lives.

Opposite below: Vessel in stoneware, hand-built, with bronze and black colour. Diameter 43 cm (17 in). By JENIFER JONES (UK), 1984. (Photo: L. Gresswell)

5. FORMS IN PROFILE

The silhouettes of vessel forms illustrated in this chapter are but a small selection of symmetrical shapes taken mainly from historical or traditional examples. Many will be familiar and recognizable as coming from Egyptian, pre-Columbian, Chinese, Minoan, Greek, American Indian or other cultures, but because they are shown merely as flat, black shapes we are able to imagine whatever variants we wish concerning their three-dimensional form. For example, one or two of the silhouettes with low, wide bodies and short, flared necks illustrated on page 210 are of 'pillow' bottles constructed from two thrown, domed or 'bee-hive'-shaped pots joined together rim to rim and placed horizontally; but their profiles might give the impression of two bowl shapes, one inverted upon the rim of the other, because the visual information available to us is limited.

It is that very limitation that can be the starting point for fruitful exploration in terms of ceramic form. It should also be understood that any extension beyond the main body of a vessel can be interpreted and executed in a number of ways. A horizontal, triangular spike projecting outwards from the wall of a pot seen in silhouette will usually suggest that it is a ridge or flange encircling the form, but, equally, it could represent an intermittent raised band, or opposing lugs, or a series of spiky additions. This is based on the assumption that the silhouette is of a form having a circular section, of course, but in fact it could also be a flattened or flask-like vessel, or the actual container section might be considerably smaller than its bulk suggests. For example, an apparently full-bellied pot seen in silhouette might, in reality, consist of a cylindrical vessel with added fins of clay which actually extend its occupancy of space. (A motorcycle engine usually has a cylinder with cooling fins attached. This configuration creates an illusion of solid mass, doubling the size overall, far in excess of the space enclosed within.)

Any abrupt directional changes in the profile of the silhouette could also be due to either additions to or subtractions from (or both) the surface of the main vessel form. We can imagine what we will and then tax ourselves further by trying to find other, alternative options that could produce the same silhouette. It is amazing how often individuals will resolve one of these black shapes for themselves in several ways and then discover that someone else has responded with totally different, yet equally valid answers. If we ask ourselves, for example, 'What if this silhouette could be the product of composite forms?' we open up our minds to search beyond the more obvious first impression.

Thrown pots, of course, can be altered from the basic form and extra pieces can be added to them or sections taken away. Composite forms can be built up from two or more thrown elements to create quite complex profiles that would be impossible to achieve in one piece on the wheel. But

The few examples in line here and overleaf represent a number of possible interpretations of two different vessels seen in silhouette. They are by no means definitive groups and the reader should be able to imagine other alternatives for conversion into three-dimensional forms.

**DIFFERENT INTERPRETATIONS OF
THE SAME SIMPLE PROFILE**

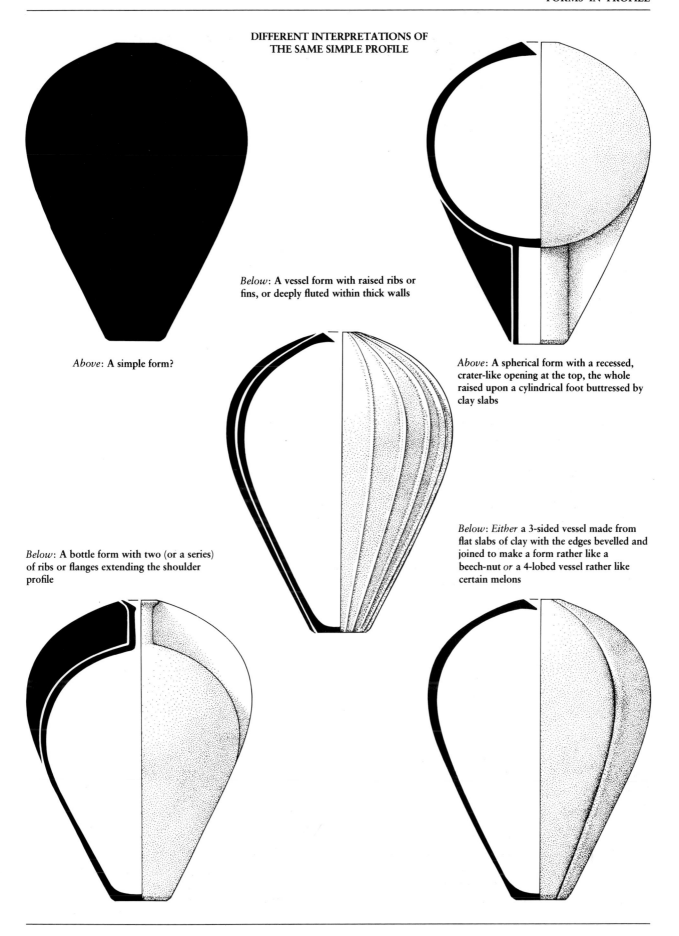

Above: A simple form?

Below: A vessel form with raised ribs or
fins, or deeply fluted within thick walls

Above: A spherical form with a recessed,
crater-like opening at the top, the whole
raised upon a cylindrical foot buttressed by
clay slabs

Below: A bottle form with two (or a series)
of ribs or flanges extending the shoulder
profile

Below: *Either* a 3-sided vessel made from
flat slabs of clay with the edges bevelled and
joined to make a form rather like a
beech-nut *or* a 4-lobed vessel rather like
certain melons

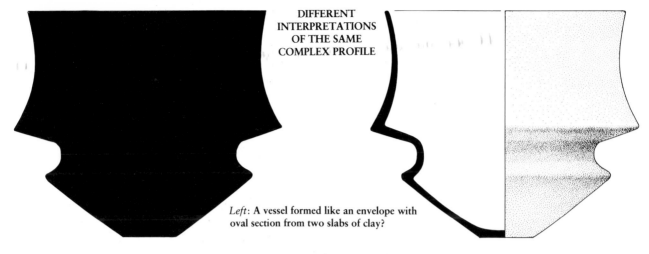

**DIFFERENT
INTERPRETATIONS
OF THE SAME
COMPLEX PROFILE**

Left: A vessel formed like an envelope with
oval section from two slabs of clay?

Above right: A wheel-thrown or coiled
vessel of circular section

Below left: A circular or oval bowl with
added wings, spikes or strips

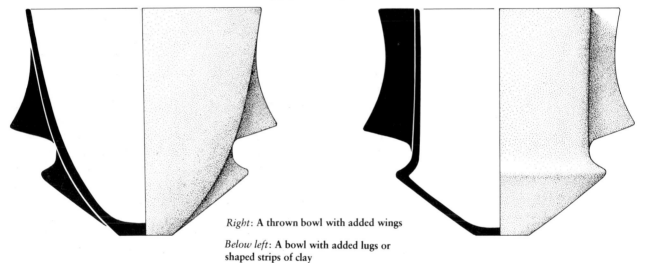

Right: A thrown bowl with added wings

Below left: A bowl with added lugs or
shaped strips of clay

Below right: A bottle or flask with stiffened
slabs applied at opposing points on the
sloping shoulders

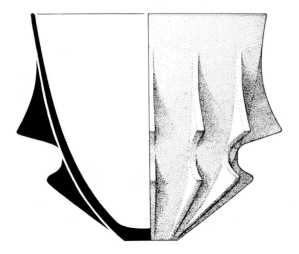

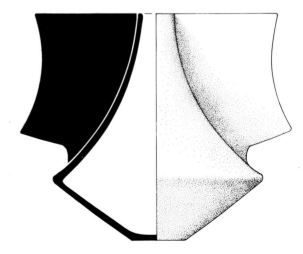

thought given to other hand-building methods and applied in the consideration of silhouetted shapes will often suggest quite radical variations that can be realized when translated into three dimensions.

Another useful option is to invert the shape and to look at it afresh. The best of the 'classical' vessel silhouettes will usually still succeed as attractive shapes when they are turned upside down. With some, that same shape may be improved by a slight adjustment to the profile at the base that 'lifts' it. (Bevelling the outer edge of the base or foot-ring of a pot serves a similar purpose in that the piece no longer appears so static.)

Apart from stimulating imaginative thought, paper silhouettes can be useful in exploring a series or sequence of related forms. Even the slightest directional adjustment in a curving profile will alter the nature of a piece while retaining its basic, family characteristics. Where the main body shape remains constant the substitution of different rims, necks or feet will offer many more options to the potter. Off-centre and multiple necks, tripod feet and similar additions provide further variants.

If several paper silhouettes are mounted together on a white background, as in this chapter, the spaces remaining between them can also provide some unusual and interesting shapes to consider; and, of course, silhouettes can be moved around and combined with others before the decision is finally taken to mount them. Multiples then become one single piece. (I am reminded of children's card games in which a number of different heads, bodies and legs can be intermixed, thereby changing the characters!) It is the immediacy of this method that is particularly attractive; the shapes can be manipulated and developed further or discarded with ease.

The strongest shapes, both physically and aesthetically, are those which possess a natural convex curvature. Their curving profile is positive and constant, with no sudden changes of direction within it from beginning to end. It may be continuous throughout the height of the pot or it may start at a point some distance above the base and culminate with a sharper shoulder line. Such curves contribute to a feeling of visual tension. Waisted forms, on the other hand, where equal emphasis is given to concave and convex curves, rarely convey the same feeling of strength. Irrespective of personal preferences concerning shape, the misplacement of one curve in relation to another in a single piece often produces an unhappy pot. Random ripples, ridges or depressions interfere uncomfortably with what would otherwise be a continuous, flowing movement. The loss of clarity destroys tension and the piece will often appear weak and flaccid.

The silhouettes included in this chapter are offered as food for thought. Some are strong and others weak. Many can be improved upon by simple adjustments of profile or the substitution of certain elements by others which may be more appropriate. Most of them are of vessels that can be seen in historical collections housed in museums, but in some cases their archaeological importance may be greater than their aesthetic presence. It is of far more value to reappraise them purely as silhouettes that can be interpreted three-dimensionally in a great variety of ways. Clearly, more extreme or extravagant expressions than these are possible within symmetrical forms. It is easier to imagine variations in three dimensions when working from silhouettes if allusions to the more familiar 'classical' lines are not too strong. Asymmetry, too, can be approached similarly through cut paper shapes. This is primarily a method to stimulate thought and feeling, but it is essential to have an unfettered mind in order to see through the obvious and beyond the first impression if one's imaginative muscle is to be truly exercised.

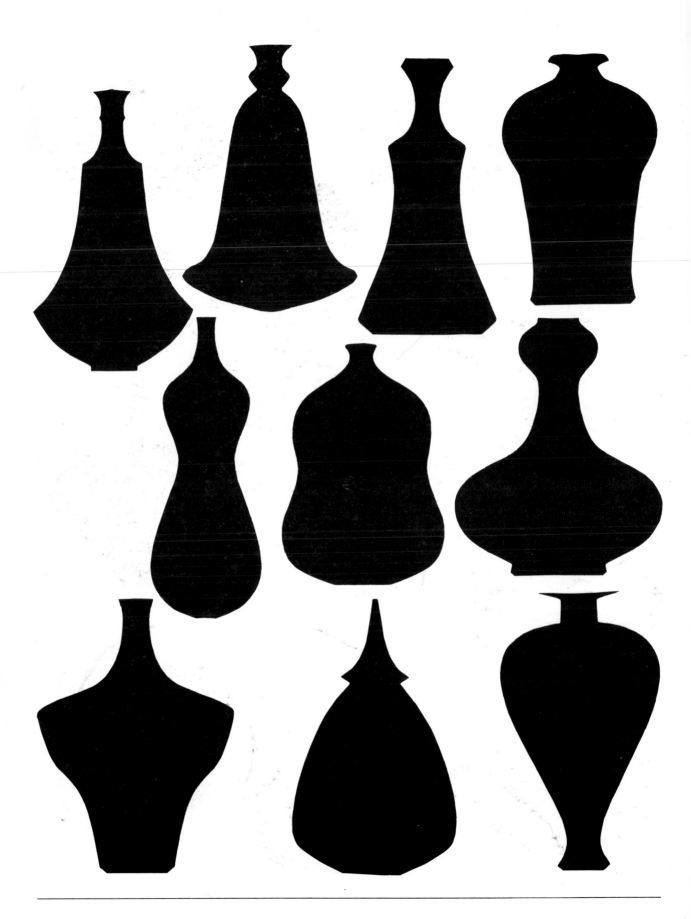

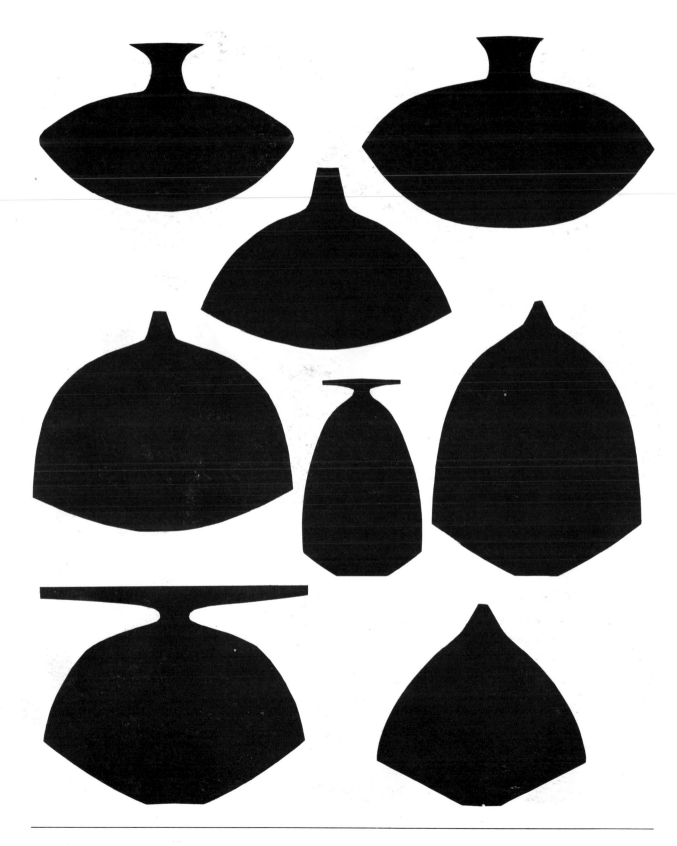

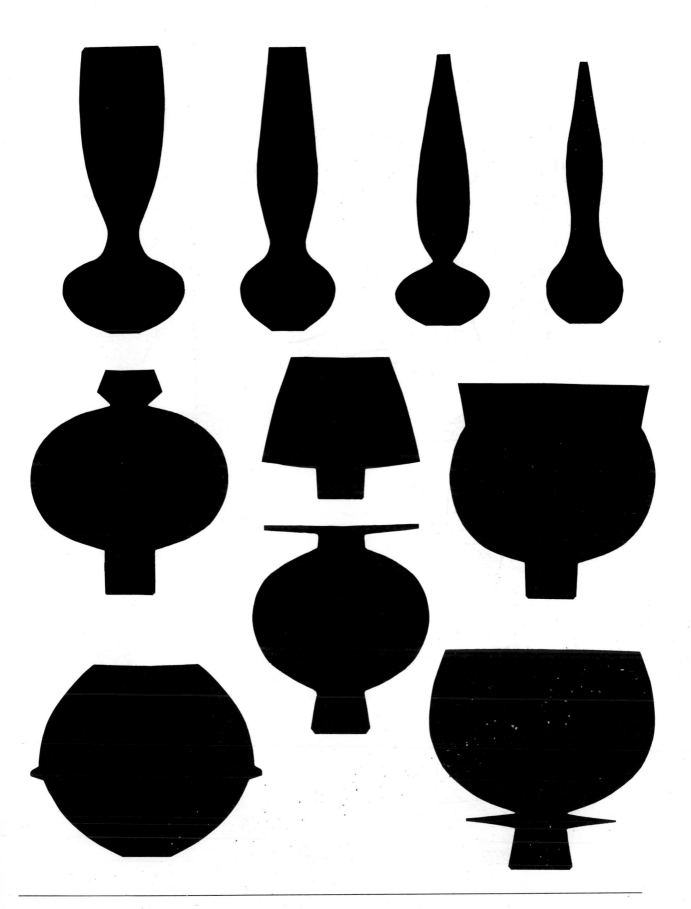

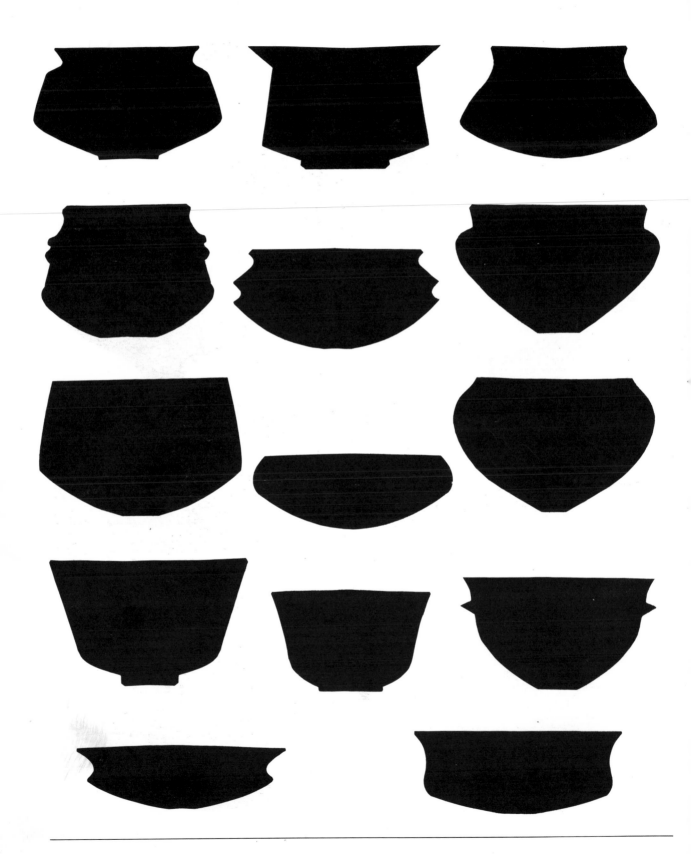

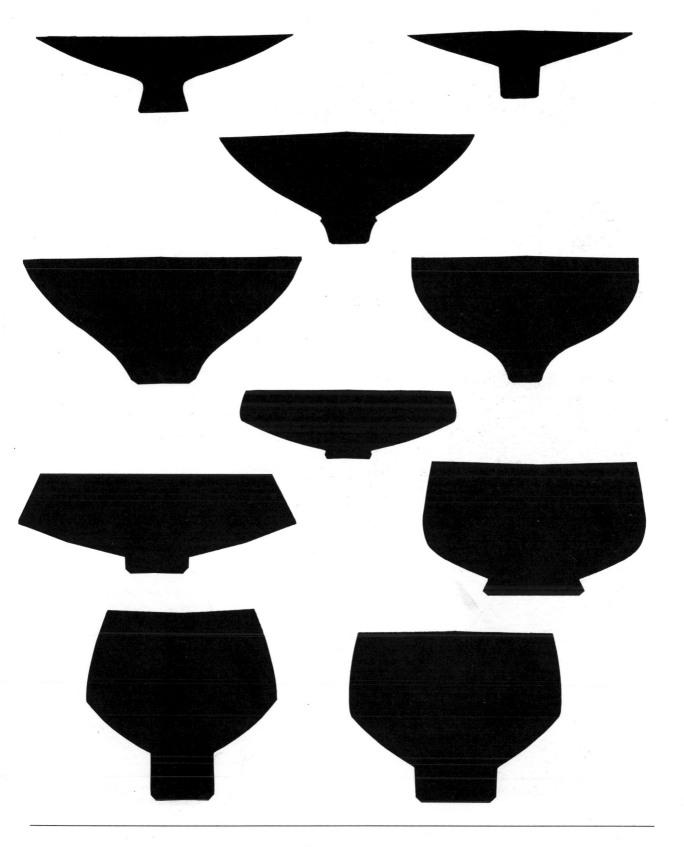

Bibliography

Billington, Dora, *The Technique of Pottery* (Batsford, London, 1966)

Birks, Tony, *The Art of the Modern Potter* (Country Life, London, 1970)

Hans Coper (Collins, London, 1983)

Caiger-Smith, Alan, *Tin-glaze Pottery* (Faber & Faber, London, 1973)

Cameron, Elizabeth, and Lewis, Phillipa, *Potters on Pottery* (Evans, London, 1976)

Cardew, Michael, *Pioneer Pottery* (Longman, Harlow, Essex, 1969; St Martin's Press, New York, 1971)

Casson, Michael, *The Craft of the Potter* (BBC Publications, London, 1977)

Pottery in Britain Today (Tiranti, London, 1967)

Charleston, R. J. (Ed.), *World Ceramics* (Hamlyn, London, 1968)

Clark, Garth, *American Potters* (Watson-Guptill, New York, 1981; Alphabooks, Sherborne)

Clark, Garth, and Hughto, Margie, *A Century of Ceramics in the United States 1878–1978* (E. P. Dutton, in association with the Everson Museum of Art, New York, 1979)

Clark, Kenneth, *Practical Pottery and Ceramics* (Studio Vista, London, 1964)

Colson, Frank, *Kiln Building with Space-age Materials* (Van Nostrand, London & New York, 1975)

Cooper, Emmanuel, *A History of World Pottery* (Batsford, London, 1981)

Electric Kiln Pottery (Batsford, London, 1982)

Cooper, Emmanuel, and Royle, Derek, *Glazes for the Studio Potter* (Batsford, London, 1978)

Cosentino, Peter, *Creative Pottery* (Ebury Press, London, 1983)

Cowley, David, *Moulded and Slip-cast Pottery* (Batsford, London, 1978)

Dickerson, John, *Pottery Making: A Complete Guide* (Viking, New York, 1974)

Fournier, Robert, *Illustrated Dictionary of Practical Pottery* (Van Nostrand, London & New York, 1973)

Illustrated Dictionary of Pottery Form (Van Nostrand, London & New York, 1981)

David Leach: A Potter's Life with Workshop Notes (Fournier, Lacock, 1977)

Fraser, Harry, *Glazes for the Craft Potter* (Pitman, London, 1973 [now A. & C. Black]; Watson-Guptill, New York, 1974)

Gombrich, E. H., *The Sense of Order* (Phaidon, Oxford, 1979)

Gompertz, G. St. G. M., *Korean Celadon* (Faber & Faber, London, 1963)

Green, David, *Understanding Pottery Glazes* (Faber & Faber, London, 1963)

A Handbook of Pottery Glazes (Faber & Faber, London, 1978)

Pottery: Materials and Techniques (Faber & Faber, London, 1967)

Hamer, Frank, *The Potter's Dictionary of Materials and Techniques* (Pitman, London, 1975 [now A. & C. Black]; Watson-Guptill, New York, 1975)

Hamilton, David, *Manual of Pottery and Ceramics* (Thames and Hudson, London, 1974)

Manual of Stoneware and Porcelain (Thames and Hudson, London, 1982)

Hettes and Rada, *Modern Ceramics* (Spring Books, London, 1965)

Holden, Andrew, *The Self-reliant Potter* (A. & C. Black, London, 1982)

Honey, William, *The Art of the Potter* (Faber & Faber, London, 1946)

Hopper, Robin, *The Ceramic Spectrum: A Simplified Approach to Glaze and Color Development* (Chilton, Pennsylvania, 1984; Collins, London, 1984)

Houston, John (Ed.), *Lucie Rie* (Crafts Council, London, 1981)

Lane, Arthur, *Style in Pottery* (Faber & Faber, London, 1973)

Lane, Peter, *Studio Porcelain* (Pitman, London, 1980 [now A. & C. Black]; Chilton, Pennsylvania, 1980)

Studio Ceramics (Collins, London, 1983)

Leach, Bernard, *A Potter's Book* (Faber & Faber, London, 1945)

A Potter's Work (Adams and Dart,

Bradford-on-Avon, Wilts., 1967)
The Potter's Challenge (Souvenir Press, London, 1976)

Lewenstein, Eileen, and Cooper, Emmanuel, *New Ceramics* (Studio Vista, London, 1974)

Lucie-Smith, Edward, *The Story of Craft* (Phaidon, Oxford, 1981)

Mansfield, Janet (Ed.), *The Potter's Art: An Australian Collection* (Cassel, Australia)

Medley, Margaret, *The Chinese Potter* (Phaidon, Oxford, 1976)

Mingazzini, Paolino, *Greek Pottery Painting* (Hamlyn, London, 1969)

Nelson, Glenn, *Ceramics* (Holt, Rhinehart & Winston, New York, 1966)

Parmalee, Cullen, *Ceramic Glazes* (Industrial Publications, Chicago, 1951)

Peterson, Susan, *The Living Tradition of Maria Martinez* (Kodansha International, Tokyo, 1977)

Pye, David, *The Nature of Art and Workmanship* (Cambridge University Press, 1968)

Rawson, Philip, *Ceramics* (Oxford University Press, 1971)

Rhodes, Daniel, *Clay and Glazes for the Potter* (Chilton, Pennsylvania, 1973; Pitman, London, 1973)
Stoneware and Porcelain (Chilton, Pennsylvania, 1960; Pitman, London, 1960)
Pottery Form (Chilton, Pennsylvania, 1977; Pitman, London, 1978)

Rogers, Mary, *Pottery and Porcelain: A Handbuilder's Approach* (Alphabooks, Sherborne, 1979 [now Collins, London]; Watson-Guptill, New York, 1979)

Rose, Muriel, *Artist Potters in England* (Faber & Faber, London, 1970)

Sanders, Herbert, *The World of Japanese Ceramics* (Kodansha International, Tokyo, 1967)

Shafer, Tom, *Pottery Decoration* (Watson-Guptill, New York, 1976; Pitman, London, 1976)

Wildenhain, Marguerite, *Pottery Form and Expression* (Van Nostrand Reinhold, New York, 1968)

Yanagi, Soetsu, *The Unknown Craftsman* (Kodansha International, Tokyo, 1972)

Zakin, Richard, *Electric Kiln Ceramics* (Chilton, Pennsylvania, 1981)

Index